Slices of Laugh

Amusing Musings
on life and family

William M. Dean

WMDbooks.com

ISBN: 9781520976846

Printed in the United States of America.

WMDbooks rev. date: November 26, 2017

for
Julia Linden

my amazing mother,
for her endless love,
patience and encouragement,
and for passing on to me her love of books.

Being ultimately responsible
for everything I write
about our friends and family
is a heavy burden to bear.

CONTENTS

I write wit and wisdom...

because what I know is laughable.

William M. Dean

ABOUT THIS BOOK

It has been said that nothing funny ever came from something that went right, which goes a long way toward explaining why every time I sit down to write about my everyday experiences, something funny comes out. However, it is through failure that we accumulate wisdom. *Slices of Laugh* is 200-plus pages of laughter and life-lessons. There's a lot of humorous fare about the major elements of my life: family, aging, writing, and Japan, but also in the mix you'll find some serious relationship and parenting advice, commentary on our modern world, thoughts on pets, health, sex, violence, and Santa—An ideal book for anyone suffering from ADHD.

Be sure to fully appreciate and enjoy every word because *Slices of Laugh* is the culmination of fifty-plus years of living and I really don't take good care of myself, so the odds are stacked against a sequel. I hope it generates some laughs, and imparts a few nuggets of wisdom, as did the life from which it is drawn.

THE e-BOOK EXPERIENCE

If you've purchased this book online, through Amazon, you can get the e-book version for free.

I regularly read and enjoy e-books. I believe that they are the future. They have made publishing more accessible for authors, lowered the cost for readers, lightened the load for travelers, and the trees are sighing a breath of relief.

However, I've spent the better part of thirty years laying out print books and magazines and, as a result, find formatting e-books frustrating. In print, I can safely work in increments of $\frac{1}{2}$ of an inch and place elements with precision. When crafting an e-book, I am delighted if a photo and its caption appear anywhere on the same page. This is the fourth e-book I have produced and I still find the standard software to be fickle and finicky. A software developer would tell you that it's not easy to construct a single document that will display correctly on every computer and mobile device. What I hear is, "blah, blah, blah, and that's why there's half a photo from page 12 on page 47." I always start out with elaborate layouts but, in the end, settle for simply centering the photos, hoping they display properly and don't interfere with the reading flow, all the while asking myself why anyone might choose to read a book on a phone.

Despite my best efforts, and depending upon your device, some photos may not display well. If you are interested, you will find full-color versions of all of the photos in this book (and it's precisely-choreographed print-book alter ego) on my book support website: wmdbooks.com.

I hope that you enjoy reading the e-book version more than I enjoyed formatting it for every computing device on the planet.

1

Dining
with the
Queen
of England

My father was a man of few words, the majority of them shouted at the dinner table. Dinner conversation was punctuated with shotgun blasts of "Elbows off the table!", "Mouth closed when you're chewing!" and "Fork down between mouthfuls!"

I think that when my father married Mom, he thought he wanted to have kids. Then he had kids, which brought order and sanity to his world much in the same way a pet ape might, while throwing feces and pulling the limbs off relatives. Arbitrarily, he drew a line at proper table manners, attempting to restore order.

After we'd finish eating in silence, my siblings and I would sit rigidly in our chairs like POWs, waiting in silence for a lull in the conversation so that we could chime, "Thank-you-for-the-lovely-dinner-excuse-me-from-the-table-please," like Mary Poppins saying "supercalifragilistickexpealidocious," but much faster. Occasionally, my father would become angry at our lack of sincerity and call us back to say it again, this time, with feeling. We'd spend about a week emoting like Hamlet, then slide back into our old routine.

Dinner times were not much fun for us, back then. I survived by receding into fantasy, imagining that I was James Bond strapped to a chair, enduring a grueling hour of torture. My brother developed a speech impediment and my sisters chose PCs instead of Macs. However, we all are well-mannered eaters.

Since that time, I have come to see good table manners as a gift from my father. At formal dinners, I frequently notice others perplexed by seemingly extraneous utensils, confused by dining protocol and distracted by trying to eat politely. Meanwhile, for me, this is all familiar and reflexive. I am in my element, except for the lack of shouting.

I am much more lenient than Dad, but do find myself repeating his old phrases and trying to whip my kids' eating habits into shape. And whenever they ask "Why?" I answer, "You must always be prepared to dine with The Queen of England." It may well turn out that if I've taught them nothing else, I've taught them to hate Queen Elizabeth II, and possibly England, as well. If she ever did invite them for supper, they'd likely decline.

The last time we visited my wife's family in Japan, my son, Noah, was 10 and my daughter, Rihana, was 8. My parents came with us on that trip, and I emphasized to the kids how strict Grampy was about table manners, so they should be on their best behavior. They rose to the occasion and the entire time Grampy was with us, I was very proud of their manners. It probably helped that there were no knives or forks, only chopsticks.

My parents returned home ahead of us and I breathed a sigh of relief thinking that my worries about their behavior at the table were over.

But, apparently, there was one rule I had neglected to mention.

*** *** ***

While I was courting my Japanese wife, Junko *(June•koh)*, she was busy trying to avoid getting married to another man. Her family had arranged for her to meet and marry into a very wealthy branch of their own family. This is not uncommon in Japan: A family without heirs may adopt a full-grown outsider male to carry forward their legacy. Sometimes, to ensure that he marries well, a bride is also arranged, in advance. In this case, a very rich uncle who'd had no children of his own had chosen a young man he thought would make a suitable heir. That young man had agreed to be adopted, swapping his birth-family name for theirs. In their perfect world, my Junko would marry this man and the union would produce male children so that the family name and fortune would be secure for another couple of generations.

Because of this, Junko was reluctant to tell her parents about me. For months, she made excuses to avoid the initial marriage-meeting until, like a prince on a white stallion, I rode in on my 1975 Tercel, scooped her up and swept her away to the extravagant comforts of my musty basement suite. This is an endless source of amusement for me and whenever we can't afford to vacation in the south of France or get a tooth filled I can't help but point to that decision and laugh. We have fun together like that. If she'd married that billionaire, I doubt they would have laughed so much about such things. So, no regrets, I'm sure.

One day, for reasons that are very Japanese, Junko's father invited us all along to a business meeting with "The Rich Uncle." On the way to the meeting, we preempted a possible rude moment by telling the kids to stop referring to him as "The Rich Uncle," even though that's how everyone in the family refers to him. The Rich Uncle took us on a tour of one of his warehouses, then one of his factories and then treated us to lunch. For other very-Japanese reasons, the business portion of the meeting was almost imperceptible, took under a minute and amounted to no more than three sentences. Afterward, we were invited to visit his home for a midday snack.

As might be expected, The Rich Uncle's house was a mansion; large and modern, yet with traditional elements reminiscent of a Buddhist temple. Walking through the large wooden gate felt like entering a movie set. The surrounding garden was intricate and perfect, the foyer huge and appointed with marble and exotic hardwoods. His wife (who,

It is much more difficult than you might imagine to act casual while snapping pictures of the snack food.

interestingly, is always referred to as "The Rich Uncle's Wife" and never as "The Rich Aunt") led the way down a long hallway to a large, glass-walled room that looked out on the garden. We sat on silk cushions around a massive Teak table and were served tea and expensive baked goods on very fine china. To be honest, being more familiar with plywood and brick shelving and milk crate coffee tables, I am easily impressed and have no idea whether all the elements were indeed as expensive as they looked or were purchased on roll-back at Wal-Mart. Still, the setting was convincing.

There was an extended silence as we all settled in and I was never more happy to have drilled fine dining etiquette into my children because it felt like we were actually about to dine with The Queen of England.

And that's when my darling daughter, Rihana, farted.

It was one of those subtle, muffled farts that might have, at any other time, been mistaken for the rustling of clothing against silk cushions or the low resonance of a saucer scuffing across polished Teak, but that particular moment of silence was so profound that it seemed to amplify that single sound into a tuba-esque performance akin to a Mac truck giving birth to farm equipment.

All eyes turned toward Rihana.

"It wasn't me!" she lied, pointing to her brother.

Fart, point and lie. A faux pas hat trick!

I felt my father turning over in his easy chair.

*"Manners are a sensitive awareness
of the feelings of others.
If you have that awareness,
you have good manners,
no matter what fork you use."*

~Emily Post

Addendum:

A reader recently pointed out to me that there is no "Queen of England" because England does not exist as a sovereign nation. There is, however, a Queen of the United Kingdom who bears a striking resemblance to the one in this story.

Parenting:Are you 2
Liam Neeson Enough?

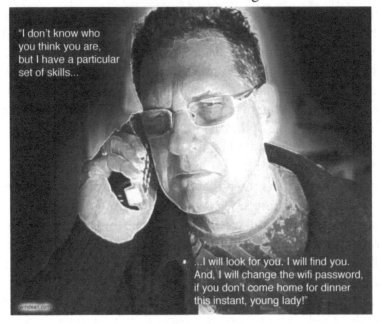

"I don't know who you think you are, but I have a particular set of skills...

...I will look for you. I will find you. And, I will change the wifi password, if you don't come home for dinner this instant, young lady!"

For me, having children seemed an easy decision. I liked children; had actually been one, in fact. Growing up, I'd been surrounded by them and enjoyed that. And it seemed a golden opportunity to show my parents where they had gone wrong. Also, sex was involved.

Ordinary people have been doing it since people first started "doing it," so I really couldn't understand what all the fuss was about. Raising children seemed like such a straightforward thing. But, as in most game-changing endeavors, after you jump in you find yourself hip deep and suddenly realize that gumboots aren't going to cut it; you're going to need scuba gear.

Reality struck early. Having sex is like entering the best contest ever and continually winning the best prize ever. Actually procreating, on the other hand, is akin to pulling the trigger on a powerful weapon aimed directly at your genitals. It turns out that sex is the one activity that regardless how much you practice and no matter how skilled you become, it in no way prepares you for success. And the success, itself, immediately seems dubious.

An incredibly forward-thinking aspect of an infant's survival skill set is to impede the possibility of competition by draining the caregivers of vitality required to further procreate. Fussiness and feedings at all hours of the night ensure that caregivers focus solely on the existing child, if they are able to focus at all. And, babies are born so vulnerable, needy and powerless that it's unthinkable that you blame them—well, you can blame them, you just can't tell anyone. So, instead, you redouble your efforts and do your best to love them even more, possibly because it's the only acceptable option. It's psychologically devious and perfect, and what keeps us from trading them in for puppies.

Most of this kind of thing I had heard from those who had gone before. Of course, I assumed that they were exaggerating. They were not. But like everyone else, I stumbled through most of it and emerged scathed, but still functional. But one thing that I have found near to crippling and was never warned about was the worrying.

I'd seen T-shirts and motivational posters that said things like; "Just Do It!" which I had, "Proud Parent!" which I was, "Become a parent. It's Payback Time!" which I think I completely misunderstood—funny word, 'payback.' But I've never seen a poster that read: "Parenting: a lifetime of worry!" Capitalism has never failed me so completely, and it's made me question the wisdom of motivational merchandise, in general.

Before children, I was easygoing, pretty much living by the mantra: "If it won't be important in five years, it's not important now." But then one morning, probably at three a.m., I awoke to the realization that everything we were doing now would affect the children five years down the road, and forever after. And my easygoingness evaporated.

Of course, when the cuddly bundle first arrives home, you worry about the obvious details: Are they eating enough? Or too much? Are they crying in pain, or just bullying? Could that stuff in the diaper be radioactive? It looks radioactive. At night, you listen to their breathing and your heart skips a beat if it's not regular as clockwork. And you keep remembering all the goldfish you owned that are no longer here. It's a nerve-wracking period during which you find out if all their internal mechanisms are in proper working order, and if you are parent enough to maintain the machine.

But then, in between legitimate fears, your tortured mind goes out into the field and picks some wild Paranoia from the other side of the fence. My first recurring and crazy worry came as a complete surprise to me and lasted for about eight years. A month into parenting, I was emotionally welded to my son, Noah, and I began to worry that we might get a call informing us that the hospital had mistakenly given us the wrong child. Would I want my genetic child? Probably. I could love two children. But surrender my little Noah? Never! It would rip me apart in a way non-parents can only imagine, or read about in high-quality books, like this one.

When I talked about this with my wife, she related a Japanese story of two families whose boys had accidentally been switched at birth. The mistake was discovered when they were about seven years old. One family was upper-middle class, had lots of rules and an intolerant, emotionally distant, workaholic father. The other family was working class, gregarious, casual, and emotionally close. The rich father believed in the idea of "upper-class blood" and, having the better lawyers, he used them to make sure that the exchange happened the way he thought best; quickly and completely. It was heart-wrenching for all involved. Both boys were heartbroken at being rejected from the only families they knew and, because the family cultures were so strikingly different, neither boy was able to make the adjustment. According to the story, in the end, the two families came to terms and decided to merge. They found houses next door to one another and the children were shared equally. No one lost a child. No one lost a parent. Knowing that this solution existed was the only thing that kept me from stashing a go-bag under the bed. This particular fear has subsided, but because it's an irrational one, it never completely goes away.

The heart churning and deeply layered 2013 Japanese film, "Like Father, Like Son" by Director, Hirokazu Koreeda, tells the story of two 6-year-olds who were switched at birth. I highly recommend watching it, but keep plenty of tissue handy.

Parenting fears are like mirrors on a disco ball: No matter what angle you look at it, there's always at least one shining directly into your eyes. They are also like Tribbles, which breed like rabbits. For a complete list of parenting fears, simply refer to Wikipedia, under "Everything." Suffice it to say that the worrying is endless and relentless.

Even the beaming health and uncommon good looks of my children cause me concern. I would love them no matter what they looked like, of course, but I am unjustifiably proud of the fact that my children are the best-looking kids ever created. I sometimes feel sorry for other parents who must see the disparity whenever their average-looking children play with mine. A logical extension of this seemingly

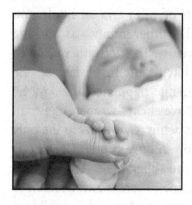

Babies remind us what beautful creatures humans can be when their minds are uncluttered by fear and insecurity.

positive belief is that my children, in particular, are powerful candidates for child snatching and I fear that I may not be Liam Neeson enough to rescue them and bring their captors to justice.

My wife often compares me to Liam Neeson, but not favorably, and so we both hover. The kids are now eight and ten years old, and only recently have we allowed them to play out of sight, in the neighbor's yard. When we do this, we open the doors and windows and investigate every silence. We're classic helicopter parents, armed with cannons that fire bubble-wrap.

It's a far cry from my childhood days when I was scooted out of doors with the parting words, "Go play in the woods and, this time, don't let the bears tear your new jacket."

For years, I've suppressed my fears and comforted myself with the thought that, "Worst case, parenting is a 20-year investment of time, money and energy, after which I can return to my quiet, carefree lifestyle." But recently, I remembered that my parents took me in for several months when my first marriage ended. I was 34, at that time. And, as I recall, I arrived bearing emotional drama and raucous friends, so that my parents' house became a busy hub of activity. They never mentioned how I shattered the tranquility of their sanctum, and twenty years passed before it dawned on me. When it's still all about you, such details tend to go unnoticed. Which leads to the startling realization that, at 34, it was still all about me.

Turns out; parenting doesn't end when they leave the nest—if they leave. And therefore, the worrying, too, never ceases.

I guess the days when it's all about me, are all about gone.

Now there's a parenting T-shirt!

Wetty Larceny

How to Steal Your Neighbor's Water

On what was surely headed toward to being one of the worst Friday mornings ever, I cleverly turned the tables and realized a dream of more than twenty years. Before you read further, you need to know that I dream small and am known to be cavalier with my use of the word "clever."

It all started at 2:30 a.m. when I got up to go to the bathroom. I turned on the tap to wash my hands and no water came out. Suddenly wide awake and frozen, with my hands well greased in soft-soap, I heard the shallow hissing of air from the faucet and realized that this is the sound you get as water falls away from the tap. "Well, that's not good," I surmised.

We'd recently had some problems with our hot water heating system, so I proceeded from tap to tap, testing, hoping for some other explanation, putting off the inevitable—checking the furnace room. When I got there, however, I was happy to see that all looked well. The system was not leaking but, of course, it was off and the pipes were cold. We have a gas boiler that delivers in-floor hot water heat, on demand. So in our house, no water equals no heat. The house was still warm but our system heats the entire cement slab under the house and it takes more than a day for the temperature to drop noticeably.

Next, I went to the windows. I assumed that it had rained because the street was wet. Then I noticed that the sidewalk was dry. I put on some shoes and ventured out. The road was covered in wet sand, which had rippled into small dunes against the curbs, like miniature beaches. Our neighborhood is built upon clay dirt. Sand does not naturally occur here, so I realized that the water main must have broken. Water pipes are buried in a trench, filled with sand and the gushing water had carried it to the surface. The entire block was wet, but there were no rivers, so I guessed that the city had already been alerted and shut it off.

I went back to bed, but was restless knowing that in a few hours, the five adults and two kids in our house would all need to use the toilets, brush their teeth and get off to work. Our new tenants had already been inconvenienced, earlier in the month, when our hot water unit suddenly died. We spent three days without heat or hot

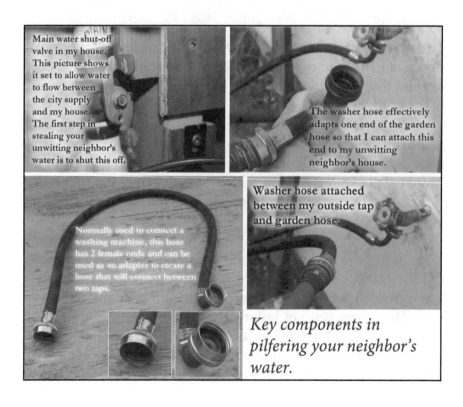

Main water shut-off valve in my house. This picture shows it set to allow water to flow between the city supply and my house. The first step in stealing your unwitting neighbor's water is to shut this off.

The washer hose effectively adapts one end of the garden hose so that I can attach this end to my unwitting neighbor's house.

Normally used to connect a washing machine, this hose has 2 female ends and can be used as an adapter to create a hose that will connect between two taps.

Washer hose attached between my outside tap and garden hose.

Key components in pilfering your neighbor's water.

How to Steal Your Neighbor's Water!

Your House

Unwitting Backyard Neighbor (on other street)

female connectors

male connector

City Water Pipe

city water shut off valve

Washer Hose

Garden Hose

STEP 1: from inside your house, shut off valve to city water

STEP 2: Attach washer hose to an outside tap. Open the faucet.

STEP 3: Attach garden hose to washer hose

STEP 4: connect hose to neighbor's outside tap and open the faucet. *Note that the neighbor must have running water.

water and I felt that having patiently put up with that, they would not appreciate being further tested.

Then I remembered!

And I realized that I had been prepared for this since 1996. This was The Moment!—The instant when I could make use of a random thought that had occurred to me way back when I was building my first house.

The thought was that if I shut off the valve to the city water supply (the valve inside my house), I could then refill my house water from another house! Our backyard-neighbors live on a different street, unaffected by our street's broken water main. All I'd have to do is connect a hose from their outside tap to one of mine, open both faucets and let their water enter my house and fill our pipes. In fact, ten years ago, I had saved an old washer hookup hose for this exact purpose.

I didn't want to wake everyone up by skulking around at three am, so I forced myself back to sleep.

At seven thirty, I got started.

I needed about fifty feet of hose and an adapter so that both ends would be female, able to attach to the outside faucets of both houses. That was what the washer hookup hose was for.

My first problem was finding that hose because it wasn't where I expected it would be. After twenty minutes of searching I gave up and decided I might somehow be able to splice together two old hoses. Shortly after butchering two hoses, I stumbled upon the washer hose. This is my life. If I were in bomb disposal, I would discover that the instruction after "Cut the red wire" would begin with the words, "But before you do that..."

I shut off the water inside my house. Then I attached the washer hose to my outside faucet, attached a 50-foot hose to that, and hopped the fence to my neighbor's house. (It probably did not look so much like a hop as a hobble—it was certainly not the "hop" of my twenties. But from the lack of police presence I safely deduced that there were no witnesses, and this is my story to tell.)

Approaching my unwitting neighbor's house, I foresaw two possible scenarios:

1) They were already off to work or still asleep, in which case I would attach my hose, turn on their water and leave a note, or...

2) they were getting ready for work, in which case I would talk to them and get permission. Hopefully, they would see that if they helped me now, I would be able to similarly help them in the future. If not, I'd head to the next neighbor's house.

As it turned out, there was a third possibility that I neglected to consider.

A light was on, so I knocked on their front door and heard a trembling voice through the wood:

"H-h-hello!?"

"Uh... Hi! I'm your neighbor, from behind, on Lancaster Street. Uh—our water main broke and I was wondering if I could attach a hose to your outside tap and get some water from there..."

"Ummm... the home owner is not in, right now. I'm not sure they'd be ok with this. Sorry."

Damn! "No problem. Thanks," I said, trying my best not to make that last word sound sarcastic.

There was only one other neighbor within reach of my hose and, lights on or not, I chose to just attach the hose and leave a note rather than risk another negative response. They have a dog, so I crept very cautiously into their back yard, attached my hose and slowly turned their squeaky faucet. No barking. The dog is old and, I'm guessing, deaf.

Excited by my illicit activities as well as the prospect of seeing my ingenious plan in action, I hopped back over the fence, ran to my own faucet and opened the valve.

Inside the house—No water.

This startled me. I went back over my theory. By now, people were starting to wake and I was running out of time. Deflated, I texted my tenants that we had no water and headed back outside to take everything apart. As I was pulling the hose back from my neighbor's yard I noticed an unusually tight kink in one of the hoses. When I straightened it out and reconnected, I could hear the water rushing through. Voila! Water for everyone. Since the boiler system was also replenished and we have on-demand hot water, we instantly had hot water, as well.

Magically, my house was now the only one on our street with running water. I was tempted to go out and water the lawn so that everyone would know. My neighbors would certainly have been startled, because I never water my lawn.

Instead, I texted my tenants with the good news, and left the system in place until everyone was out of the house. Then, while detaching my hose, I bumped into my neighbor who told me that he was happy to have helped and thought my fix was surprisingly clever, which I chose to take as a compliment.

In all the years since this solution first occurred to me, you might wonder why I never asked a plumber about it. Well, first of all, it never came up. Secondly, I was afraid they might tell me that this is an old and well-known hack, from way back; that it's common knowledge to plumbers. It was my original thought and, I believed, an inspired leap. I didn't want the outcome handed to me; I wanted to find out on my own. This is so "me," and it's why I never read any of those self-help books everyone keeps pushing on me. I'd so much rather puzzle things out on my own, even if I have to stumble through disaster to get there. For some reason, "owning" the solution gives me a deep satisfaction.

This is one of those rare occasions when my inspiration actually paid off and I was ecstatic. It is also one of those moments when, unable to contain my enthusiasm, I recounted my adventure to my wife and kids and received blank stares in return. "Should I get you a gold star, Daddy?" said my nine-year old daughter, who suddenly seemed to have mastered sarcasm.

They are completely unimpressed because they don't know, or care, about plumbing and can't appreciate the leap of genius that had to happen in order to think the original thought, or the dedication required to allot space in my brain for twenty years, or the foresight involved in saving a piece of hose for ten years, or the good fortune in being able to find that hose when it was needed. They don't know that this solution would never occur to the average homeowner. And they don't understand how a genius-type-thought of this magnitude can make up for so many gap-moments: Like that time when you suddenly forget your best buddy's name, or when you walk into a room and can't remember why you went there, or when you put the cat in the freezer, or forget the baby in the car seat in the parking lot at the hardware store. This makes up for all of that! Well, at the least, it goes some distance towards.

I wish I had watered the lawn.

Dad's I.T. Guy

In every life, there comes a point where a new technology overwhelms you. That is the point where you officially become "old."

A lot of people instantly got old when they couldn't figure out how to get rid of the flashing 12:00 on their VCR's. More were thrust into old age when phones became so advanced that their least impressive feature was phoning. For me, it might be when everyone lives in empty white cubicles with fully augmented reality and I refuse to give up my flesh and blood wife, or my plastic lava lamp—depends on the day. It'll definitely happen if people begin getting USB ports sewn into their necks. I'm pretty happy with the orifices I have, thank you.

"Old" happens when change comes too fast and goes too far.

My father became "old" at 70, when he got his first computer.

It's not a matter of intelligence.

At 78, he walked into a party where fifty other guests, including myself, had spent the better part of an hour scratching our heads over a picture-word puzzle. He took one glance, said, "The answer's 'Tumbler,'" as if it were no more of a challenge than picking Ronald McDonald out of a lineup of Mallard ducks, grabbed a beer and sat down seemingly preoccupied with keeping his drink from foaming over.

Beyond his family, he truly loves only three things: TV, sports and gambling. He's now eighty, but as physically fit as a sixty-year-old with a mind agile enough to regularly conquer Sudoku and Crosswords. He golfs at least twice a week and plays floor hockey against forty-year-olds. He's a good enough poker player to amass small fortunes in online credits without spending a dime and regularly places near the top in worldwide tournaments. Perversely, when he goes to Vegas, he plays the slots and Keno, games that require the least skill and offer the worst odds. He only seems interested in beating odds that are overwhelmingly stacked against him. This may explain fifty-plus years of marriage to my mother.

He's brilliant when he's motivated but, to my mother's frustration, has spent the better part of his life unmotivated except by sports and gambling. He is gregarious and very popular, but largely unconcerned by what others think and is unapologetic if his frank assessments or opinions make others around him miserable. He is also not much concerned whether his assessments and opinions happen to be accurate. I think he sees them more as social experiments than social comments.

As he's aged, he's adopted the outward demeanor of a crusty old curmudgeon but has always remained active, astute, and one of the most deeply contented people I know.

He is also one of the most frustrating people to do a favor for.

I once cleaned his gutters and had to listen to him grumble the entire time about the dirt falling into his garden. Until then, I'd always thought a garden an appropriate place for dirt.

My parents have a huge hedge in their back yard and once every few years all of us siblings get together and trim it, which requires scaffolding and specialized trimming tools. Each time we do this, he spends the day whining about damage to his lawn, trimming too much foliage and leaving a huge mess, though none of these things has ever occurred.

Of course, my siblings and I all feel that we owe our parents a huge debt for all the things they have done to help us through life. And to his credit, in the end, Dad always makes it clear that he is genuinely thankful for our help. But things go so much smoother if he's busy golfing.

Other than socializing, TV, sports and gambling my father feels that most other activities are an unnecessary burden, so if he has to do something like house repairs or maintenance he aims for hair's-width perfection in the vain hope that, if done right, he will only have to do it once in his lifetime. He applies this philosophy indiscriminately, which is why whenever he mows the lawn he does it in different directions, thrice over. He's hoping that this job, well done, need only be done once a year. Both my mother and the grass refuse to accede to his logic.

About twenty-five years ago when my brother-in-law was new to the family but safely past the line for an annulment, I volunteered him to work with Dad at one end of a new fence-line while my brother and I worked together at the other. Our part went very smoothly and after a few hours we had installed about eighty percent of the new fence and came upon my Dad and brother-in-law still working on their third post. Dad was bent over the hole which was, apparently, not yet deep or straight enough. He had an old hammer and chisel and was bashing away at solid rock, three feet beneath the surface. My brother-in-law stood holding the 8-foot fence post, gazing aimlessly skyward, frustrated by the knowledge that they would now have to fill beneath the post so that it would not be too short for the six-foot panels. When he saw us, he did not smile.

The question of who is going to be my father's IT guy has been a hot potato since that same brother-in-law made the mistake of giving my father his first computer, many years ago. It was a PC and, at the time, I was never more happy to be a "Mac Guy." Since then, my brother-in-law has continued to donate his business's retired PC's to my father. But this year, there were no PC's in the system when my Dad's suddenly died— probably suicide. However, my little consulting business had an Apple iMac that it no longer needed. And that's how I became my father's IT guy. It's nice to see my brother-in-law smile again, but bittersweet.

GUI (graphical user interface) concepts like desktop, file folders and files are useless analogies for my father. If you ever saw his actual desk's top, you'd quickly understand why. As in real life, he files everything on the desktop. If a file accidentally ends up inside a file folder, he considers it irretrievably lost; an assessment that is not without merit.

The inevitable phone-line support calls are difficult because, regardless of his crossword prowess, his descriptive ability is severely limited, proving that I get my writer's mind entirely from my mother's side. To him, a monitor is a TV. The computer, its RAM memory, the hard disk memory, any tangle of wires in the vicinity and, often, the Internet are all just "the computer." Words like reboot, program, app and scrollbar have as much meaning to him as Gangsta Rap lyrics in Sanskrit. He dislikes anything that works differently from his first computer, so being able to run two programs at once is a fault, not a feature. Also, his first computer was a PC, so he hates Macs—more intensely, with every update. "It's just like Apple to waste resources on a stupid concept like multitasking."

This is the foundation upon which I am to build a functional IT relationship.

My first approach was to put aliases, buttons and links everywhere thinking that he could activate his favorite programs and websites in any of four ways. This was a mistake. A week later, when I checked in, he had stopped using the computer because it was too slow. There were fifty-seven tabs open on Chrome.

Dad: ...and then there's this cheap aluminum keyboard...
Me: Cheap? You mean, compared to plastic?
Dad: It has too many keys.
Me: It's the alphabet, Dad. Same on all keyboards.
Dad: What's with these ef'n keys.
Me: That's "Fn" keys... they're function keys.
Dad: What do they do?
Me: That depends on what you are doing on the computer at the time.
Dad: I'm hitting the damn key, is what I'm doing. Useless. Take them off.
Me: Uh...

It's been tough slogging, but we've made some progress. Not in the IT department—we're no further ahead, there—but we've established a routine that ensures the problem gets dealt with as quickly as possible.

Dad: Your crappy computer's busted again. I get some sort of message about errors.

Me: What's on the screen right now.

Dad: Lint.

Me: Is the computer on?

Dad: Yes.

Me: But no picture?

Dad: No. I shut it off.

Me: You shut off the picture? Does that mean the TV-part is off?

Dad: No. That's on. There's a yellow light.

Me: Turn on the computer.

Dad: What do you mean, turn it on. I've got a yellow light.

Me: No, that's just the TV-part. You need to press the button on the box-part. You'll know it's on when you see a blue light.

Dad: Ok. . . . There's a blue light.

Me: Great. What's on the screen.

Dad: Lint.

Silence.

Me: *[Because this is not my first time.]* Is the blue light actually lit up, or are you just telling me that you finally spotted it?

Dad: It's there.

In Dad-speak, this is adequate confirmation that it's not lit.

Me: Did you press the "on" button?

Dad: I'm still pressing it.

Me: You've got to let go.

Dad: You never said that.

Me: How have you been turning it on for the past two months?

Dad: I never turned it off.

Me: Is it on now?

Dad: There's a box in the corner and all hell below that. The thing doesn't work anymore and when I press the other thing all I get is crap.

Me: What's that sound?

Dad: I'm trying to make it go.

Me: Is that the mouse clicking? Why is it clicking so much?

Dad: I'm clicking on everything to get it going.

Me: We should go slowly here.

Dad: Are you kidding? It's slow as molasses!

Me: How many windows are open now?

Dad: Windows, boxes, lines... There's junk everywhere.

Me: Is there an error message?

Dad: There was but I clicked it away.

Me: What did it say?

Dad: Something was an error.

Me: Yes, but what?

Dad: I don't know... something about "insufficient."

Me: Memory?

Dad: I don't know. Illegal, invalid, restricted... something, something, "wager not placed" something, something.

Me: Were you playing on an online Casino when it first came up?

Dad: What the hell else does a person do with a computer?

Me: Were you trying to make some sort of bet at the time?

Dad: I don't know. This box came up and I couldn't see the slots anymore. Your crappy computer broke the Internet. I want my old one back.

Me: Your old computer was barely compatible with electricity.

Dad: It worked better than this.

Me: I'll come over.

Dad: Great. Bring a trowel.

Me: Sorry? What?

Dad: One of those gutters you "supposedly" cleaned is clogged again.

Me: I did clean it, Dad. That was three years ago.

Dad: You should probably bring a ladder, too. And a bucket so you don't get dirt in my garden.

Me: See you in a few minutes.

Dad: There's a six-pack in the fridge.

At last!—A foundation upon which I can build a functional IT relationship.

The True Artists in My House

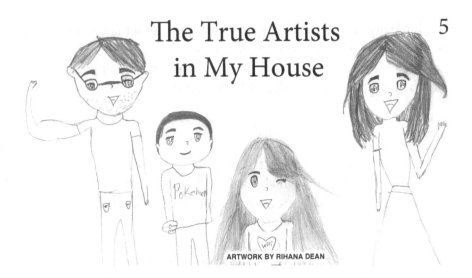

5

ARTWORK BY RIHANA DEAN

My house has artists the way others have silverfish.

My kids are mini art-factories, pumping out scraps that become priceless masterpieces, once they scrawl on the words "I Love you, Daddy." I, on the other hand, spend a lot of time pumping words into novels and blogs hoping to create masterpieces without having to resort to kissing up to my parents.

And then, there's my wife, Junko. *(June•koh)*

The other day I stood watching her dissect a head of lettuce so that she could individually wash each leaf before preparing a salad and a couple of thoughts passed through my brain much in the same way that light doesn't. First: The disquieting notion that my wife was smiling while dissecting a head. This was immediately followed by the thought that I eat fewer bugs than the average person.

According to the first article in a Google search, the average person consumes between one and two pounds of bugs per year. This means that, by now, I would have eaten my wife's weight in bugs had she not been preparing most of my meals for the last 12 years. As it is, I have consumed one and a half of my children's weight. Why I see this in terms of how many of my family members I have eaten, I do not know. Suffice it to say, I am a survivor and you do not want to go down in a plane in the Andes with me on board.

Once, when we were dating, I took Junko to a fancy local restaurant, whose name I will decline to mention. Actually, my memory is a bit foggy on this detail. It may have been another fancy restaurant whose name I will decline to mention. Yes... more likely there. At any rate, as we tucked into our first course, I noticed a small pile of black dots accumulating at the edge of Junko's salad plate.

> **Me:** Are those peppercorns?
> **Junko:** Bugs.
> **Me:** Wha-a-at? There can't be bugs in a salad from a restaurant as fine as this one which I will decline to mention the name of.
> **Junko:** Actually, I've never had a salad in a restaurant which did not contain a bug.

I check over both shoulders, lean forward and whisper, conspiratorially, "Do you think it's because you're Japanese?"

Junko, lips pressed, gives me that exasperated look that seems to ask, "Are you four?" It made me simultaneously feel foolish, yet proud to be a Canadian.

> **Me:** Well it's just that I've never had a bug in a salad. Ever.
> **Junko:** You just ate one a few minutes ago. And last week, at that other restaurant that you always decline to mention the name of, you ate several.

I flip another leaf and sure enough, there's a tiny black beetle swimming in Balsamic and goat cheese, with a touch of ginger and honey. When I say "swimming," I mean dead.

> **Me:** Why didn't you say something?

After twelve years of marriage, I can now answer that question. I have come to realize that, for Junko, my suffering is an endless source of amusement.

Junko is the primary cook in our household. In our early years together, she made a few meals that were so exotic and unfamiliar (these are euphemisms) to me that I was tempted to ask, "Who ate this first?" It wasn't the food itself that put me off—Junko's an amazing cook and her food is always skillfully prepared—it was just the look, texture, smell and flavor I couldn't handle. But I realized that if she could leave Japan for me and accept a largely Western diet for the rest of her life, then I should be willing to at least try everything she cooks, at least once.

This is why the first time she served fresh water eel I made myself eat every last scrap even though I thought it tasted like rancid worm rectum. I hate rancid worm rectum. When I looked up from my plate, I noticed that Junko had eaten everything except the eel. I asked her if she was saving it for last. She said, "I think it's off." When I asked her how she could silently watch me choke down an entire fish without mentioning this, she giggled. Admittedly, her giggle was cute and I did not die, but it's no wonder I have trust issues.

Once, when I had an ingrown hair she offered to pluck it, noting that she plucks her body hair all the time and assuring me that I would hardly feel it. She tweezed the offender and tore the inner lining from my left nostril. My eyes watered and I dance around the house, screaming into my fist for about twenty minutes. She laughed the entire time and encouraged the kids to join in.

To be fair, she also laughs when she hurts herself. Still, it's weird.

If everyone were like this, standup comedy would be radically different and involve medieval surgical tools.

When I look around our house at the few things that she keeps out for display, I am reminded of all of my treasures, which she has carefully packed into boxes for display in our attic. Admittedly, the house looks a lot better than my bachelor pad—though I do miss my boobie beer stein and the Kirk and Spock salt and pepper shakers.

I am the conservative, even-tempered, straight arrow type who might just as easily have become a chartered accountant living in obscurity, as a writer living in obscurity. And now, as I stand watching Junko scrub each lettuce leaf and pat them dry with a towel I realize that, of the two of us, clearly, she is the true artist, applying her talents to the fading art of homemaking.

The FLYN System:
A Band-Aid Solution

6

Darth Vader would have been much scarier if he'd said, "Luc, you're just like your father!" None of us want to become our parents, but eventually, the inner child recedes and that inner parent leaks out. And, one day, we find ourselves telling our own kids to stop arguing or so help us God "we're going to turn this car around," and we realize that life and karma have conspired to make us clones of our parents.

My father has a great memory but, for some things, he staunchly refuses to use it. Instead, he writes copious notes about things he worries might be too complicated to remember—from booting up his computer to resetting the furnace. When I was young, these notes would be written on yellow legal sheets and taped to the various objects to which they pertained. He had a scribble-pad at his office desk, and another on the end table beside his easy chair, in front of the TV.

As life progressed and technology got more complex, my father also moved forward. He upgraded from yellow lined sheets to little yellow sticky notes. He bought a home theater system about a year ago and now it's just about impossible to pick up his remote without getting a paper cut. If you visit his house and he wants to make sure you don't forget something, my father, who assumes that every mind works like his, will stick a sticky note to your glasses, or even your forehead. I hate being labeled. "Before being seen in public, remove sticky from forehead," I once wrote on my hand.

A close friend, who always disliked Dad's clutter of Little Yellow Notes, dubbed this the FLYN system. I leave it to you to figure out what the 'F' stands for.

I never subscribed to my father's FLYN system. I decided early on to rely on my memory. Then I had children and, in the confusion, forgot where I left my memory. Technology saved me. My smart phone has a note making function that I've come to depend upon to make sure that I don't forget to tie my shoes, or remove my glasses before bed. But now, my phone is so full of reminders that it often seems more convenient to fight to recall something, rather than sort through the various notes. Also, that 'TO DO' list is depressingly long.

Today, I was surprised to catch myself pasting a little yellow sticky note to the front of my phone. But the larger shock was to realize that this is not an isolated incident. It's a habit. I once had a note on there so long that the adhesive lost its 'stick.' I had choices: I could have completed the task, written a new FLYN, or added the note to the electronic collection on my phone. Instead, I used scotch tape to stick it back on.

Resistance is futile.

Slices of Mike

Mike's Camera

I don't worry much about global warming or animal cruelty because my heating bills keep climbing and most of the animals I've encountered have been quite gentle, or food. My brother, Mike, is not like me in this way. He became a vegetarian entirely because of such concerns. He's an engineer, but lives as naturally and sustainably as one can while driving an SUV and spending ten hours a day in front of a CAD terminal, designing A/C systems for shopping malls. As engineers go, he's practically a hippie, albeit a clean-shaven one with tightly cropped hair, wearing a tie and blazer.

He has a little point-and-shoot camera, which in its default mode can identify faces and take pictures when people smile. Strangely, it refused to take pictures of my bubbly, perpetually smiling daughter, Rihana. Eventually, she concluded that she had lost too many teeth for it to recognize her smile. I thought that this was a startlingly astute deduction for a seven-year-old, which made me smile—at which point Mike's camera took my picture.

Mike enjoys long hikes in the countryside and it occurred to me that if he were ever attacked by a voracious, man-eating Grizzly his

31

little point-and-shoot would almost certainly start snapping off a grand series of crisp shots of those 3-inch canines. These would become treasured keepsakes by which we could all fondly remember him and his camera.

All That and a Bag of Chips

One night, Mike, invited me to meet him and go see a movie. I met up with him as he got out of his car and was throwing a few things into the trunk. Among them, I noticed a large bag of potato chips.

Me: What's that? Your dinner?
Mike: Floor hockey chips.
Me: Huh?
Mike: Once a week, I play floor hockey and the guys and I go for beer, afterward. I keep the chips for then.
Me: Why don't you just order food at the pub?
Mike: It's not about that. Sometimes I worry that I might be a little over the limit, when we leave…

He explained that once, twenty years previous, he had been stopped at a police roadblock, blew close to the limit and received a roadside suspension. He had to park his car and lock it up. They took his key and he had to walk home, at two in the morning.

Mike: It was a long walk, and raining, and I only had a light jacket. It was miserable.
Me: I still don't get what's with the chips.
Mike: I just couldn't help thinking that if I'd had a bag of chips, it would have been better.

My brother Mike is one of those people who will often surprise you with an alternate point of view, but it is rare to find fault in his logic. Case in point: Floor hockey chips.

After reading this article, if you ever see six empty screw holes inside the drum of your clothes dryer, you will know what I now know:

A: That there should be a screw in each of those holes,

B: that your dryer is broken, and

C: that you are about to blow three hours of leisure time out of the water.*1 *(see footnotes)*

My wife, Junko *(June•koh)*, is Japanese*2. Junko's family does not really celebrate Christmas. For them, New Year's Day is the big deal. The Japanese idea is that you want to enter the new year, the way you'd like it to proceed. To me this suggests her in lingerie and me in a bottle of scotch. To Junko, it suggests sterilization—thankfully, not in the way you're thinking.

---

*1. *This does not include time spent swearing at inanimate objects or bandaging cuts from razor-sharp metal edges.*

*2: *"My wife is Japanese." This is a very useful catch-all sentence. I use it when one of the kids does something inappropriate or when I pay with coupons. If your wife is Japanese, you should use it, too. It's one of the perks.*

On the 31st of December all Japanese "celebrate" by rigorously cleaning everything in sight. At least that's what Junko told me and what I believed until the year we spent Christmas in Japan. That's when I learned that my wife is a cleaning fanatic, even by Japanese standards. She'd scrub the white off of rice, if she could, and does not consider a window to be truly clean until birds start bouncing off of it.

Previous to this revelation, on the 31st, we'd clean the house from top to bottom, armed with toothbrushes, razor blades, screwdrivers and crowbars, for those hard to reach spaces. We moved fridges and stoves and took apart things like shelves and small appliances to get at the nooks and crannies. Another tradition was that every year, after about five hours of this, I got grumpy and quit.

Tired and grumpy was how I entered the new year. Junko entered it disappointed and unsatisfied. And, too often, the year would proceed the way it began.

On that eye-opening New Year's Eve in Japan, her father spent a couple of hours tidying up and leisurely organizing his tools in the garage. He whistled a lot. Her sister-in-law was humming like a princess in a Disney movie, as she lightly dusted the furniture. My two teenaged nephews brushed their teeth, then watched TV. There was no grunting, groaning or muttering of swear words, and the rest of the day was spent lounging and visiting with friends. I realized that an arduous New Year's sanitization of every possession is not a Japanese thing—it's a Junko thing. The jig was up!

She has since scaled down my New Year's Eve chores to only a couple of hours' work. I now insist on a list in advance, so that I know what I'm up against. Sometimes, I will start a few days ahead in order not to spoil my holiday. This year, my list included cleaning the dryer of all lint as Junko had noticed that lint was gathering in behind the drum.

I want to take a moment to point out that I am actually quite handy. I build stuff, can change my own brakes and oil, have repaired everything from vacuum cleaners to furnaces and done a lot of renovating. None of that has ever taken a nasty turn.

In this case, however, I was lulled into a false sense of security by the prevalent, modern notion that evolution is going about it all wrong and that being a moron should not lead to harm. The six-inch-deep blow-up kiddie pool I bought last summer has a warning label: "No Diving", and our toaster's manual advises users not to butter the bread *before* it's toasted.*3 Naturally, I assumed that screws inside the dryer that were so accessible were meant to be removed.

A faint voice inside my head was telling me that doing so was a bad idea, but I ignored it thinking that it was just the ghost of resentment at having chores on my holiday. I figured, the worst-case scenario might be a wasted minute or two. What the voice was trying to say was that even if I removed the screws, it is obvious that the panel cannot be removed because the dryer vanes are in the way and this should be a warning that those screws are not meant to be removed. *But they were so accessible and invitingly shiny! And the voice was all whiny and condescending.*

When the first screw came free, I immediately sensed that something heavy had shifted. I have no idea why I carried on. I am normally a very cautious guy. When I'm not sure how something is going to pan out, it is my policy to do nothing. This is why I don't play the lottery and, by extension, why I must waste precious holiday-time tampering with a dryer.

Removing the second screw had no effect. But when the third screw came out, a large metal disc behind the drum fell onto the heating element. The coils glowed fiercely for a few seconds, then shorted out with a blinding flash and a crisp *pop!* The coils were now broken and welded to the rest of the dryer. My wife pointed out that we were lucky that I, too, had not been welded to the dryer. She was probably concerned for my well being, but it's equally likely that she was thinking that the constant clunking sound of my body tumbling around whenever she did the laundry would eventually become tedious.

My five-minute cleaning job had just expanded to fill the day.

I am ashamed to say that I did some cursing. But, I didn't curse my wife or the dryer. I cursed the engineer who designed it and who decided to place six temptingly shiny screws where I could so easily get at them. Then I cursed myself for a while. That was fun.

3: Sadly for me, there is no warning on a package of Doritos to tell you that the pointy ends are sharp. And nowhere on the Band-Aids package does it mention that they won't stick to the roof of your mouth.

Our stacking laundry is located in a very tight closet and locked in place by shelving on one side. In order to extract the dryer, I had to remove the shelves and lift it off the washer, pull it through a doorway designed to admit anorexic field mice and gently place it on our kitchen floor in the middle of the most travelled intersection in the house, thereby impeding the only access to the kitchen, bathroom and the back door.

While I did this, my wife went online and looked up a schematic for the dryer, then asked me why I had not done that first. My mood now much enhanced, I looked over the schematic then watched a quick repair video on YouTube, which naturally led to checking out pictures of Ellie Kemper, then jokes from The Office.

Eventually, I began to disassemble the dryer. The kids were suddenly parched and had to get glasses of water from the kitchen. You should know that young children have nothing between the mouth and their rear ends. Internal organs and such grow in later. So, after about thirty seconds, they had to use the bathroom. This cycle was repeated repeatedly, each time with a "How's it going, Dad?" as they passed.

"Just ducky," I said, having objectively determined that this moment was just right for a lesson in the art of sarcasm. They gave me a thumbs-up, each time.

I called around for replacement parts and was fortunate enough to find a new heating element, nearby. Thirty-five dollars and another hour later, I had vacuumed every internal inch and had the whole thing back together.

It's much more difficult to lift a stacked dryer back into place because half way up, you must adjust your grip lower down on the unit. It took me another hour to place it, attach the vent, put back the shelves and replace all the useless crap that we normally store on those shelves.

"Ok. Your damned dryer's 100% lint-free, now!" I was wise enough to not say.

Incidental to this, that same morning, my wife was cleaning the fan above the stove and stripped the screw that keeps the blade in place. I made an ingenious repair involving a drill and hack saw and put it all back together. The fan now sucks perfectly, but wails like a banshee—or sings like Kate Bush, depending upon your taste.

I went to the garage to get more tools and the door handle came off in my hand. I fixed this too. We now pry the door open with a stick.

Lately, when I go online and search DIY repair, Google automatically redirects me to a professional.

OK, "Mr. Fixit" -- Now can we call a plumber?

Four Original
Halloween Stories
You Can Tell
in Sixty Seconds

9

Just before Halloween, I was driving the kids to visit their cousins and they asked me to tell them some scary ghost stories. The skies were ominously dark, sooty clouds roiled above while gale force winds buffeted and torrential rains drummed against the car. By the glow of the dashboard and dull thumping of windshield wipers, I spun these horrid tales…

Me: Once, there was a ghost couple who were married. The wife-ghost went out shopping and racked up thousands of dollars in credit card debt! Sca-a-ary!

Kids: Dad!

Me: Once upon a time, there was a little ghoul and her very best ghoul friend. The ghoul-friend said something very insulting and the little ghoul got ALL of her feelings hurt!

Kids: Da-ad!

Me: Once, there were 3 ghost friends who went out haunting. The first ghost passed through a wall, followed by the second ghost, but the third hit the wall with a Thump! and fell to the ground.

The other two came back and hovered over him. Then one ghost said, 'D-dude, I-I think you're ALIVE!' A-a-ah!

Kids: Da-a-ad!!

Me: Once upon a time, there was a struggling author who hired a gho-o-ost writer to finish his book. The gho-o-ost writer did a terrible job and missed every deadline. The author's publisher dropped him and he fell into obscurity and died.

Kids: Dad, can we listen to music?

The quickest way to silence a kid is with a disappointing performance.

*** *** ***

A Somewhat Related Story...

One day in the middle of winter our furnace was acting up. We have fireplaces enough to heat the house in an emergency, but our furnace is a combination unit that supplies all of our hot water, as well as heat. When it started arbitrarily rationing our hot water, I began to worry because our furnace is the fancy kind about which every plumber who ever sees it for the first time says things like, "What the hell is that?" and "Do you have some sort of manual for this thing?" or "I've never seen one do that before." Though they all sound distinctly different, they all mean the same thing: This is going to be expensive.

I've been in the furnace life support game long enough to know a few tricks and managed to coax mine away from the light for about a week, but my efforts were losing ground and it was becoming clear that it was going to take more than a few hearty thumps on the chest while shouting "don't you die on me!" to keep it going much longer. It appeared to me that I was going to have to buy a very expensive gas valve and call a gas fitter to achieve another remission. We had reached a tricky point in this furnace's life where the idea of pulling the plug was beginning to have some appeal. I started pacing the house while deciding whether to repair or replace.

Our house is not very large, so the only effective way to pace is by strolling through the kitchen, living room and hallway, moving slowly to avoid furniture, home school projects and toys that litter the path. After a few go-rounds, I became peripherally conscious of my children tracking me and giggling. But, I was distracted and barely noticed. When finally I awoke from my reverie, I realized that they had closed the drapes and shut off the lights and were alternately stalking then scurrying away from me. When I asked them what they were doing, they said that they were pretending I was a wayward spirit and that they were Ghost Busters.

I asked what they would do if I suddenly died and came back to visit them as a ghost. Their answer: "Flee in terror and hit you with plasma cannons!"

So I guess I won't do that.

10

A while back, I took my wife out to dinner at an up-scale restaurant. The Deep Cove Chalet has all the attributes you look for in a fancy place: French chef named Pierre, gorgeous, secluded waterfront location, fantastic food, parking lot filled with Mercedes', Porches', Lamborghinis, and my 1994 Ford Aerostar. Also, snooty waiters.

Normally, I might order scotch or white wine, but that night I just wanted a humble beer.

Me: Do you have any Japanese beer?
Waiter: Excuse me?
Me: Japanese beer. You know: Asahi or Sapporo?
Waiter: [sighing condescendingly] Sir, we are a French restaurant.
Me: Are we? Oh. I see.

I quickly skimmed the wine list. "I guess I'll just have a glass of the Argentinian Malbec, then."

I'm pretty sure he spat in my food—I've heard that French cuisine is all about the sauce.

*** *** ***

About six months later, it was getting close to my wife's birthday and I came across a Groupon that startled me. I thought it was for the Deep Cove Chalet. Actually, it was for the Brentwood Bay Inn—an easy mistake to make, if you're me, because Brentwood Bay and Deep Cove overlap on the map in my mind. On every other map in existence, they are about six miles apart. Just one of the many reasons more people rely on Google maps than on me.

So, in my mind I'm thinking Deep Cove Chalet, but the rest of reality is insisting that it's the Brentwood Bay Inn. I'm extremely stoked to find such a deal and my state of denial is so great that it does not occur to me that the Deep Cove Chalet French Cuisine Restaurant would never participate in something so gauche as an online coupon, let alone a four-course sushi tasting event.

Instead of wondering why a French restaurant might host a sushi event, I'm thinking I've really scored big because, firstly, Junko loves Deep Cove Chalet, secondly, she loves sushi and, as an added bonus, I get to ask that waiter for a Japanese beer and I'm dying to hear him choke on his snooty comeback, while serving sushi.

I eagerly snap up the deal and even buy an extra, so that I can be a real hero.

Of course, upon opening her birthday present, my wife was quick to point out my error. The gift was not a big hit—at least six miles short of that, in fact.

My wife is thrifty and efficient and considers buying at retail to be an extravagant waste. She peels stamps off of our mail and reuses them, extensively uses coupons and will return sub-par items to a garage sale. She absolutely hates it when I waste money, which is a bit of a shame as it's one of my defter skills. She has taught both of my kids her thrifty ways but they love it when I waste money because berating Dad is good clean fun and watching Mom berate Dad is better than watching Sponge Bob.

So now we're obligated to go to a restaurant that neither of us would have chosen—though, technically, I did—and my wife's primed to be skeptical and hypercritical, going in. The sushi may not be cooked, but I'm pretty sure my goose is.

Scotch, neat. And make it a double!

My only comfort is in knowing that my 1994 Ford Aerostar will not look as out of place in this parking lot as it did at the Deep Cove Chalet.

I am disappointed that I won't have the pleasure of one-upping that snooty French waiter.

Also, my Groupon-ing privileges have been revoked.

This round goes to you, Snooty Waiter. But mark my words: You have not heard the last of me!

That might have been the scotch talking.

*** *** ***

It's two years later: My brother-in-law, Mark, has been forced to trim staff and I am let go from the family business. This comes as no surprise. My efforts there have not been producing fruit for several months and I am very frustrated but unable to make the obvious call, and resign. When he finally does, I am relieved. Mark is a very loyal friend and suffers such guilt that he decides, as a grand farewell, he will treat me and Nancy, a co-worker who is retiring, to an evening of fine dining at The Deep Cove Chalet.

I prepare for my rematch with The Snooty Waiter by dressing in a suit and tie and, this time, I use deodorant. I'm no longer driving the 1994 Ford Aerostar. I've upgraded to a 2004 SUV which I wash and polish (and scrape candy off the kids' seats and, strangely, wipe tongue tracks from their windows) until it looks near new. Smoothly, I pull in between a jet-black Jaguar and a fire-red Porsche Boxster, confident in the knowledge that my car is as shiny as the ones next to it and that no car is immune to a squeaky fan belt.

After we're seated, our waiter introduces himself and I am a little disappointed to find that he's an entirely different individual from last time; young, and looking far less snooty.

Waiter: Would anyone care for a drink, to start?
Mark: I'll have the 25-year Bowmore.
Waiter: Excellent choice, sir. And you, madam?
Nancy: I'd like to try a glass of the Chartron-Trébuchet Chardonnay
Waiter: My pleasure. And you, sir?
Me: What kind of mixed drinks do you have?
Waiter: All of the classics, sir.
Me: Great! I'd like a Slippery Nipple.
Waiter: *[his eyebrow arching so high it disappears beneath his hairline.]* I'm sure. But, as I said, we only serve the classics.
Me: Ah. Ok, then: Blue Hawaiian.
Waiter: *[sighing through his nostrils]* The classics, sir.

He's suddenly become much snootier than his years. *Is he even old enough to drink? Has he ever actually tasted alcohol?* I briefly consider how I might put him in his place by asking how much he makes, then remember that I'm here because I no longer have a job.

I don't dare take a third stab at ordering something I actually want. Instead, I say, "How about a glass of the house white," casually, as if I'm not in the habit of purchasing wine by the glass, pizza by the slice or dental work in installments. But even I know that "house white" is a cop-out; a white flag.

"Of course," he says as if he'd expected that, all along. No "my pleasure," or "excellent choice," or even a "sir." I can read his mind: *"No matter how remarkable the menu, a chimp will choose the banana."*

"You know what? I'm exceptionally thirsty, tonight…" I lean back in the chair and look out the window, surveying the manicured lawn and the beach, beyond, as if only minimally aware of the waiter's presence. "Bring me the whole box," I say while stirring the air with my hands in a whimsical, dismissive gesture, as though ordering wine were a dreary formality.

"I'm speechless," he declares, then walks away.

Yes! That's one for the primates! I smile like Bond, James Bond. "No doubt, at these prices, they don't get many people who order a whole box."

"No doubt," says Nancy.

My wine arrives. It's in a bottle, not a box. I pretend to not be surprised or disappointed, but then I notice that it isn't even a screw top and can't refrain from shaking my head a little and uttering a soft "tsk-tsk." I had intended to drink a glass or two and take the rest home. The table has been turned, yet again. This Snooty Waiter is wilier than I'd calculated. But if he thought that most of the bottle would be wasted, then he, too, has miscalculated. I'm healthier than most my age, 190 pounds, and am used to stronger stuff. I don't need a screw cap. I can drink the entire bottle. I do wish I liked wine.

Two hours later, when we are leaving, I surprise the waiter by referring to him as "my frère from another mère!" while I have him clamped in a bear hug. "I have enjoyed our time together, mon amigo!" I say, pressing the entire contents of my wallet into his palm, insisting, before he can protest, that he take it all. "Farewell, and bon frites!" I am waving and blowing kisses to all the other patrons as my companions pull me out the door.

At noon the next day, I stumble from my bed to the bathroom. It's while brushing my tongue that I recall snippets of the previous night. I rush to examine my wallet and discover that, thankfully, it still contains the five-dollar bill, however, eighty-five cents worth of Canadian Tire money, a McDonald's coupon for free hash browns, and a receipt from Super Cuts are missing.

"Another one for the primates," I say, but very softly.

Footnote:

Just in case it is not obvious: The Deep Cove Chalet is certainly one of the very best dining establishments on Vancouver Island, and I am thankful that it exists so close to my home. The food is amazing, the prices are reasonable, the portions; surprisingly generous, the setting; serene, and the waiters are probably not as snooty as I recalled. One word of caution, however: Some of the customers can be annoying.

Adventures in Couponing

Years ago, I remember watching reality TV featuring extreme couponers and thinking to myself that those people were crazy. Now, I'm married to one and yes, she's crazy, but that has little to do with coupons, and damn! but we save a lot of money.

If you are ever in a cash register line-up in Victoria, BC, Canada and see a cute Japanese woman with a cartful of groceries and a fistful of coupons in deep discussion with the cashier, best to move to another line. That's probably my wife, and she is a serious couponer who firmly believes that schooling cashiers and store managers is time well spent.

Looking at a single coupon, you might not think that the savings could be significant, but the trick is in combining it with other coupons, and in-store specials. Many manufacturers offer brand-wide discounts that can be combined with their other, product-specific coupons. If the store's shelf-price is particularly low, you can save more than one hundred percent on your purchases! On occasion, we've bought groceries and been paid in cash at the till for our trouble. More often, we pay a small amount and later receive a rebate check, by mail.

Basic requirements…

To really make a dent with couponing, there are three basic requirements:

- time enough to search flyers and the internet for deals,
- money enough to purchase things ahead of your needs, and
- space enough to stockpile.

An Internet connection is becoming essential as more and more manufacturers have stopped printing paper coupons, now only offering them online. There are also apps you can download to your smartphone to help you find deals as you shop.

Technically not essential, but something that will definitely improve the experience, are loving and understanding family members who are flexible regarding the products they consume, and patient while you shop.

In her native country of Japan coupons are not common; the Japanese prefer points•cards. So my wife, Junko *(June•koh),* was shocked, ten years ago, when she got her first taste of couponing. It was shortly after the birth of our son and we were going through so much formula that I was thinking that we needed to have a frank discussion about just how tall a child really needs to grow.

Junko was shopping, one day, and noticed a pallet of baby formula at a discounted price. The deal was made even more attractive by a brand-wide, percentage-off coupon she had spotted in a flyer. I'm sure that she was skeptical that they would allow the combined discounts on the entire batch, but she read the coupon over carefully and could find no limitations. She must also have been scared, pitting her second-language skills against a native-English-speaking cashier. But curiosity and greed won out. She called me and asked if it was ok for her to spend a few hundred dollars to purchase the entire pallet load. I was shocked by the total amount and laid down the Imperial Husbandly Law: "Absolutely not!" Three days later, I came across a pallet of baby formula in storage at the catering company, which is our family business. I should not have been surprised. My wife has a rather lengthy criminal career, in the eyes of Husbandly Law.

At the time, I was pretty upset and rehashed it in my mind, every time I fed the baby. It's a testament to Junko's calculating ability that we ran out of formula about one month before the last baby bottle.

Much later, during a discussion with other parents, I finally came to appreciate what Junko had accomplished with that bulk purchase. While other families spent $25/can (Cdn.), or more, Junko got ours for five dollars each.

By the time that initial supply ran low, Junko was a seasoned couponer, able to purchase more at a similar rate. Raising two babies requires about two years of bottle feedings: That's at least 160 cans. On this product, alone, she saved our family a minimum of three thousand dollars!

Meanwhile, Junko had moved on to diapers. At one point, our attic was filled with boxes of Pampers; $35-boxes that she'd managed to get for less than seven. She never bought a single diaper at full retail and accrued enough that we ended up giving away the last few boxes. Online, I found some statistics on typical diaper usage and calculate that couponing saved us about $1600—not to mention possible savings on our heating bill, with a hundred boxes of Pampers insulating the attic.

When Zellers, a large retail chain, went out of business, Junko used coupons on their already deeply discounted items. She is a curious mixture of demure and dauntless, and calmly created a huge traffic jam at the cash registers manned by a newly trained and frenzied liquidation sales clerk. Applying her coupons she bought a $100 stroller and a $150 highchair at 70%-off, and left permanent creases in the foreheads of two managers. These items lasted us through both children. Junko diligently kept them clean and in good operating condition so that, once our children outgrew them, we were able to recoup the entire investment during our annual garage sale.

Because of her, we raised our babies to toddler stage, practically for free. I tell my second-born that if we hadn't got a discount on the first child, we wouldn't have been able to afford to have a second. It's funny because she thinks I'm joking.

The Stigma:

Before Junko showed me the light, if I had ever given coupons any thought at all, the thought would have been that I was averse to using them. Forced to justify this, I might have pointed out the inconvenience of collecting, carrying and using them to save insignificant amounts of money. But mostly, it was the embarrassment of having people think that I might be so poor that I had to use coupons.

My attitude changed abruptly the first time I witnessed her purchase brand-name bacon at a dollar a pound while the next person in line paid five. I thought about how it would feel to be that person, and my embarrassment vanished, replaced by pride. Suddenly, I wanted to tell everyone I knew how much money my clever wife was saving us.

But, of course, most people are still hesitant to use a coupon. Junko has offered other shoppers her extras, which is a great way to create an awkward moment from scratch. The strangers tend to stare, bewildered, unable to properly assess the value of what she is offering and, usually, politely decline. Conversely, however, if a cashier applies a coupon automatically, as they do at the London Drugs in our area, customers would never consider refusing to accept the discount—no different than they would accept a special price marked on the shelf.

It's all about interaction. These days, people do not want to interact with their cashier. They just want to pay and go home. And, when it comes to coupons, many cashiers don't look forward to the interaction either, as it can often be a brow-furrowing experience; deciphering the limits of the offer and assessing how it might interact with other offers, as well as store policy.

I, too, was resistant for years, but now I'm smug. For me, it has become clear that coupon savings are the reason we can home school our children and vacation in Japan every three or four years, without financial consequence. I don't shop often, but now, before I do, I always ask Junko if she knows of a deal or has a coupon that might apply. Also, I let her know in advance when I'm thinking of purchasing something so she can keep her eyes peeled for specials.

Our children have been raised to save. Their keen eyes are quick to spot in-store specials and though they don't clip coupons, they do check the flyers if they have their eye on something. They have Christmas and birthday money to spend, but neither one would ever consider purchasing a toy at full retail. My son once waited two months for delivery of a video game, direct from Japan, because it was $5 cheaper than at Toys-R-Us. When I was a kid, I couldn't even wait for Jell-O to set.

The Challenges:

When it comes to couponing, Junko applies all of her considerable cunning and will not be deterred. When I see the determination, attention to detail and meticulousness with which she maps out her shopping itinerary, I know that if she wanted it so, I'd already be dead. So, no sense worrying about that, but, also, maybe I should buy some flowers on the way home from work today.

Before I understood the magnitude of the savings, I could not fathom why successfully cashing in a coupon seemed to make her happy. But, *"happy wife, happy life,"* so I was patient, if not encouraging. A couple of years later, her methods evolved from just cutting coupons out of newspapers and flyers to looking them up online and submitting receipts, electronically. She was consuming hours, each day, hunting for new coupons, researching how those could be combined with in-store promotions and studying store policies in the eventuality that a cashier might refuse to cooperate. Her savings went from half-off the occasional product, to checks arriving in the mail,

February, 2016. Above: Total cost, $15 (Cdn) Below: Total cost, $30 (Cdn)

paying her for purchasing! At first, as couponing started consuming her hours, I was concerned, but I soon went from tolerating her new-found hobby, which sometimes

meant we had to make random and inconvenient grocery stops during family outings, to praying that she never stops.

It should have been obvious when she decided to marry me that she likes a challenge. I think, Junko views couponing as a challenging game, with money as the prize. And, for a traditional Japanese housewife, there can be no greater incentive than saving the family money. *(In Japan, typically, the wife is the financial manager, handling all the important decisions, including when to buy and sell the family home, and doling the husband a monthly allowance.)*

For Junko, there certainly are challenges. English is her second language. She's fluent, but even so, understanding the fine print on some of these promotions is like deciphering a law text. Which brings up the next challenge: Many cashiers and managers are not so fluent and need further education in their own language. When she feels it may be necessary, Junko prepares by bringing with her printouts of store policy and coupons with key phrases highlighted. Before shopping, Junko often spends an hour organizing her coupons, her itinerary and her strategy, working out which coupons can be combined, where the savings will be maximized and how to present it all at the cash register, including counter-arguments, should there be resistance.

In spite of all of this preparation, sometimes things do not go smoothly at the till. If the store is unwilling to allow her discounts, Junko will easily and politely relent, but she will also abandon her coupon purchases. In this day and age where everyone considers their time to be precious, store personnel are often unprepared for this and I have witnessed their shock as Junko leaves the store empty-handed, and their unexpected loss of time and sales sinks in.

If you think about the coupon system, you will realize that it must work for both the manufacturer and the store or else they would not offer it. When you redeem a coupon, the store sends it to the manufacturer who repays the store for the discount. There is no loss to the store. The manufacturer considers it an advertising cost and hopes to transform a couponer into a loyal customer. Somewhere in an office in Los Angeles or New York, some advertising executive has calculated it all out and decided that the benefits outweigh the expenditures, including the cost of obsessive-compulsive, bulk-purchasing couponers. But many cashiers and store managers do not understand this, and resist redeeming coupons. Admittedly, in this computer-paced age, with multiple offers on the table, things can get complicated. Still, there is no reason to rant or cry about it. But sometimes, they do.

At one Shopper's Drug Mart outlet, Junko purchased three jars of pickles. She could have cleared the shelves, but she imposes what she considers reasonable limits on herself. Combining a coupon with the in-store sale price, it came to pennies a jar. The cashier cried, telling her that they would go out of business if people kept doing this. Junko was embarrassed and said nothing, but she was thinking that they should consider raising their price on pickles. Regardless, the store will be reimbursed. The cashier's concern assumes that management has not given this any thought, and in regards to a national chain like Shopper's Drug Mart, this is naive. Last January, when Junko returned a roll of wrapping paper that she'd purchased before Christmas, for 80¢, the manager threw a tantrum, smashing the roll against the countertop and throwing it across the floor while surprised shoppers gawked. Apparently, he was angry because he'd just bundled up all the leftover wrapping paper and returned it to the manufacturer. Perhaps he should have considered his store's two-week return policy. I suspect that the problems at that particular location run deeper than simple issues of retailing.

Superstore has a policy that if the in-store price marked on an item is incorrect, they will give you $10 off at the cash register. Junko quickly realized that our local branch was lax in making sure their shelf prices matched the flyers. One day she found a product that was mispriced in this way. It cost less than $10 and, of course, she had a coupon. The manager was called and reluctantly gave her cash for purchasing. Junko waited a week and returned to find that they still had not changed the shelf price. She bought another. Again, the manager was called and was even more reluctant to hand over the money. Two weeks later, Junko found the shelf price unchanged and bought the item for the third time. The manager freaked out and told her that this was the last time she would honour the coupon. What's weird is, all they had to do to solve the problem was change the shelf price. Junko feels that they should either change their store policy or get their act together and she is merciless on this issue, regularly finding other mispriced items and going through that same manager, every time. There is little doubt that she is truly hated by that particular manager. Incidentally, two weeks after all of this, the price was still unaltered. My theory: This store is banking on the consumer's reluctance to call them on store policies they advertise to attract customers. In the long term, this is not a winning policy.

But, sometimes, the staff can be on her side. During the brief time that Target was in Canada, they had some strange policy of selling things at full price for a few months, then putting them on special at prices so low that it was ridiculous, presumably to clear shelf space. When these prices were combined with coupons, the deals were so spectacular that Junko went there almost every day and the cashiers came to know her. They were so impressed with her deals that they'd strike up conversations about her methods. Some planned to make similar purchases for themselves. Everyone at Target was friendly and helpful, including the guy running the hot dog cart outside the main entrance who asked her out for coffee. She tells me that she declined.

Junko was heartbroken to see that store close their doors, but I joked that she had, singlehandedly, couponed Target out of Canada. She did not find this funny. Too soon, I guess. While Junko mourned, Target's bean counters were doing their "happy dance." I'm sure there are still board meetings during which they watch security footage of Junko shopping their profits away, as a training exercise.

Conundrums and dilemmas...

You might not think so, but in couponing there are dilemmas which may or may not be moral. It's hard to say as there is little mention of coupons in the Bible, Torah or Quran, and the Dalai Lama has been conspicuously silent. The closest I've seen to moral guidance was a fortune cookie that said, "Today are golden human nicety. Choose Daily Special for $1 off! Your lucky number is G," but after eating the Daily Special, I don't put much stock in that.

The ethical grey area starts back with the very definition of a coupon. By one definition, a coupon is a discount offered by the manufacturer, targeted at people who have not yet tried their product in the hopes that they will become loyal customers. But for this plan to work, most loyal customers must pay full retail while newcomers get a discount. A darker view is that it is a kind of pyramid scheme that robs loyal customers in order to attract new ones. If all goes as the manufacturer plans, the loyal customers will never see the coupon and the newcomers will fall in love with their product and start purchasing it, even when they don't have a coupon. Once they are loyal to the brand, they will, in turn, be "robbed" to finance the next coupon-fishing expedition. It's the opposite of the idea of rewarding loyalty. But obviously, it works, because not only do manufacturers keep on issuing coupons, they are issuing them in greater numbers than ever before.

The government has its own ideas about coupons, considering them another form of taxable income. If those coffers had their druthers, every consumer would be required to declare coupons on their taxes. Presently, this is impractical, not to mention that it would effectively undermine the entire coupon model. But they want their piece of the pie and so here's their compromise: If you have a coupon for 100%-off an item, you will pay sales tax on the full retail value. This seems rather arbitrary when you consider that if the store offered a 100% discount at the shelf, there would be no tax. It would be considered a free giveaway, and, moreover, a tax-deductible expense for the retailer. Consequently, there are times when it's more economical to purchase an item at the cheapest advertised retail price than to apply a coupon and pay tax on the regular retail value.

And, on a smaller scale, there are personal dilemmas.

Junko shops every day and thus is rarely "scooped" by other couponers. She has ample opportunity to clean the shelves of items she finds valuable. But she doesn't, feeling some obligation to other couponers as well as to the store; allowing it to attract other customers with the discounted products. If there is a pad of coupons attached to the store shelf, she will help herself to a reasonable portion of them, but will not take the entire pad, as some do.

But what about coupons that are actually attached to a product? That's trickier.

Say a 25%-off coupon for bacon is attached to skin cream. Is it ok to take one without buying the skin cream? Is it ok to take them all? Or should you only take the ones attached to products that you buy?

For most, the initial reaction is that it's wrong to take the bacon coupon unless you purchase the skin cream. Obviously, the manufacturer does not care, otherwise they would put the coupon on the inside of the packaging, or incorporate it into the label so that it cannot be removed. For those who really just wanted skin cream, there is no loss if the coupon is missing. The worst case is that those that wanted, both, skin cream and bacon don't get a discount. There can also be a downside for the store if it does not sell bacon. In that case, taking the coupon removes the extra purchasing incentive from the skin cream and the store might lose skin cream sales, recouping nothing through bacon sales. But, the upshot is that few, if any, are negatively affected by missing coupons.

But it can get even trickier, still: What if you are using the coupon to purchase another flavor of the same item? The first time Junko encountered this particular coupon-dilemma was with hair dye. The blonde dye had a discount coupon attached to it. But she wanted brown. She peeled the coupons off the blonde and used them to purchase the brown dye. She did not clear the shelves, but did buy 20 boxes: Male hair dye. Not one of her subtlest hints.

Junko still does not have a firm policy on such coupons. Most people won't use coupons and are unaffected, but she doesn't want to steal from other couponers, nor does she want to negatively impact the store. She feels that she must apply limits in order for coupons to continue to work for everyone involved: consumers, stores and manufacturers. It's a matter of long-term sustainability.

Being perfectly fair to all concerned is a sensitive matter. And the typical initial reaction is often the exact opposite of the reality.

I have also noticed this to be true when we give a gift that has been acquired using coupons.

It is well known to our family and friends that Junko is a couponer. They know that she regularly gets things like brand-name hair products, cologne, perfume and makeup, chocolate bars and movie tickets for free—or close to it. Each Christmas, she creates generous gift baskets for all the adults composed of these products. It's never been said, but I suspect that even though these are very practical and expensive products they are not appreciated at their full value because the perception is that they are free. Well, first of all, they are not free. Even if they cost us little, or nothing, Junko spends hours working to get these products. And, secondly, as Christmas gifts go, they are by far the most thoughtful ever exchanged among the adults in our family because she thinks about these people and their needs on a regular basis, all year long. If you ask her, you will find that she has a very good reason for giving every item in a basket to that particular person. If it's the thought that counts, then her gifts are extremely valuable.

These days, we're all pretty sensitive regarding our carbon footprint and, in this respect, couponing will not make you any sort of hero.

Many of the items we get are one-time-use, disposable or sample-sized products. Junko once came home with 300 sample-sized packages of Zantac heartburn medication. None of us have stomach issues, and so, we gave a lot of it away. Each cardboard container held a plastic and foil strip that held only three pills. Why did she buy so many? Because when she submitted the receipts to an online coupon site we got more money back than she paid because of a Zantac rebate that applied even to these 3-packs. It was good for us, but not so good for the environment as all of that packaging had to be recycled.

At the height of her mania for her newfound hobby, Wal-Mart had a policy that allowed Junko to purchase groceries at great savings. In order to accomplish this, she picked up dozens of their free, full-colour product magazines, ripped out the coupons she wanted and dumped the remaining forty-plus pages into our recycle bin. She operated similarly with other free magazines and newspapers that are distributed around our city. For a time, she even drove around to fast food restaurants asking for flyers from their day-old city newspapers. Managers were happy to be relieved of the excess paper.

Magazines and flyers are not printed in one's and two's, so all of this printed matter and associated packaging is going to end up in a recycle bin somewhere, regardless whether couponers take them. However, if there were no couponers, the print runs and the associated environmental impact might be smaller.

These days most coupons and discounts are offered online and printed out at home, if they are printed at all. When Wal-Mart extended their price matching policy Canada-wide, Junko went online and found flyers in small eastern towns, printed reams of advertisements as proof, and price matched against obscure corner store specials. During that time, she brought home meat, cheese, fruit and vegetables, often paid nothing, or got money back at the cash register. She then spent days cooking up a storm, converting the raw ingredients into frozen meals. Only the environment and our recycling collectors suffered.

Myths...

Many people believe that items purchased with coupons must be off-brands, expired or damaged. Largely, this is untrue. Junko purchases the same things as everyone else. Occasionally, she will buy a chocolate bar or bag of potato chips that may have expired, but only because we believe that those dates are more of a marketing tool than a warning.

For the most part, we ignore dates on fertilizers, detergents and toiletries, judging that they may become a little less effective over time, but not critically so. Largely, this has proven true, though we have had a couple of surprises. Liquid drain uncloggers and liquid fabric softeners coagulated and became unusable, after two or three years. So far, those have been the only losses, and they were minor because Junko is careful not to overstock as she always has new deals that could use our limited storage space.

Junko's stockpile storage closet. We also have a garage and attic filled with less-volatile products.

Some think that couponers gratuitously stockpile. Perhaps, some do; but not us. Junko never buys items that we will not consume. Sometimes, we've had to be creative in order to use large quantities with nearing expiry dates. For instance, when she purchased thirty pounds of cheese we grated it and froze it for use in cooking, because cheese goes bad quickly and, once frozen, it only regains its original texture when melted.

Downsides, and the unexpected...

For us, Junko's couponing has been a completely positive thing. In fact, our little family has become dependent on it. If she ever decided to quit, I'd probably have to get a second job or pray that the books I've written start selling—yeah, it'd be the second job. But there are some downsides:

Whenever I make a purchase, whether it be a stick of gum or a load of gravel, I am aware that Junko would have spent less for the same thing. She is also aware of this and tends to grimace whenever I come home with something store bought.

- We eat more frozen products than we used to.
- Our recycle bins are always overflowing.
- We had to buy a larger freezer.
- We have a walk-in closet, half of the attic and much of the garage dedicated to stockpiling.
- My nephew decided that it would be fun to jump all over 700 rolls of toilet paper. For two years I thought of that kid every time I went to the bathroom and had to use paper that did not roll smoothly because the cardboard tube had been crushed. Harbouring that much resentment toward a six-year old is an uncomfortable feeling.
- We don't always get the brands we grew up with. So, often we don't get the flavors we prefer.
- Junk food is one of the easiest and cheapest items that we can

Over concern for my health, I asked Junko to reduce the junk-food acquisitions, so this cabinet is about half as full as usual.

get. Our junk-food cabinet is the malnutrition capital of the world. Also, we have a junk-food cabinet.

- The day after Valentine's Day, Easter, Halloween and Christmas the junk-food cupboard overflows to the walk-in closet.
- Some things are more potent than you might imagine. We once stored boxes of fabric softener sheets in the same room as everything else and, within weeks, the smell had infiltrated some of the food, including sealed boxes of crackers and breakfast cereal. We've since relegated all of the offending products to the garage. Two years later, the storage room still smells like Bounce, which is a pleasant smell in the air, but an unpleasant taste in the food.
- In order to get extra coupons, Junko has borrowed the identity, email addresses and physical addresses of everyone in the family, close friends and our tenants. I particularly resent the coupon notifications on my smartphone that make me think, for an instant, that I am popular enough to receive a text.
- Our son and I had grown up on Kraft, somewhat-unnatural, peanut butter but our daughter was just starting solid food when Junko purchased about six jars of Adams all-natural peanut butter. I didn't like having to stir the oil back into the thick paste before I used it, and neither of us boys really liked the taste. Consequently, household peanut butter consumption plummeted and those jars lasted about four years. Finally Junko purchased another jar of Kraft. Our son and I were elated, but our daughter, who had only known the all-natural brand, didn't like it. We now have a family whose peanut butter tastes are so far apart that we have to buy both. A similar thing happened with Miracle Whip and Hellman's Mayonnaise.
- Because she can always get them cheap, we use baby wipes as napkins. They are particularly convenient for road trips but are mildly disconcerting on the dining room table.
- The most useless things Junko ever collected for free were pesticides like Off! and Raid! We have two dozen cans and no one we know wants to use any of it. We'll sell them at our annual garage sale, along with all the excess candy we think we will never be able to eat. If you have a sweet tooth or an infestation, you'll want to come to our garage sale. I may use that line on the signage.

- Junko bought me about a dozen sticks of an antiperspirant labelled, "clinical strength." It's so powerful that my armpits have friction burns and I swear that it sucks the moisture out of my mouth. Also, the back of my hands sweat. It is practically impervious to soapy water and I am tempted to use a scrub brush, each night. I suspect the label was meant to say, "clinical trial." I'm the only one I know who is hoping for a chilly summer.
- Once, while we on our way to visit a relative, my wife made me stop the car so that she could go dumpster diving to retrieve coupons from old newspapers. To be fair, it was a paper recycling dumpster and not a garbage dumpster, but people can't tell that when I show them the video on my smartphone.
- Since she began couponing, buying gifts for my wife has become near impossible. First of all, if she really wanted it, she would have found an incredible deal and purchased it on her own. If she has not done this, then she really doesn't want it. Further, we both know that she would have gotten a better deal than I did, and, though she's smiling, she views this gift as a waste of money she could have saved.
- Although she manages incredible savings on everything from toilet paper to plant fertilizer, so far, no deals on big screen TV's or computers. She did get a microwave, coffee maker, waffle iron and a digital camera for the kids, at huge discounts, so she's moving in the right direction. I'm going to put a bug in her ear regarding Scotch, as well.
- She once brought home eight bricks of unsalted butter. That's when we discovered that I have limits: You do not tamper with the butter or the popcorn!

When it comes to shopping, I am resigned to being the John Watson to my wife's Sherlock Holmes; following along behind, shaking my head in disbelief, and chronicling to friends and family her adventures in couponing—while munching on potato chips. I have been put in my place, transitioning from tolerant to awestruck to dependent. I may be the breadwinner, but she's the one who brings home the one-dollar bacon!

War Stories from the Dandelion Fields

12

In the future, when scholars recount The Great Dandelion War of 2016, my name will figure prominently.

Whenever I mow the lawn, my kids refer to it as "harvesting the Dandelions" and, truthfully, if Dandelions were a cash crop, I'd be rich and wouldn't have to mow my own lawn. And this would be best because I've got a gangrene thumb. (I also have a purple index finger, but that's from an unrelated Do-It-Yourself incident.) I'm the most ignorant gardener there ever was, but my wife has no interest in it and so, because she maintains the interior of the house, by default, I maintain the yard.

In 2016 I decided to mount a counter-offensive against invading Dandelions.

It's not that I don't like Dandelions. In fact, I think they are a beautiful plant and, personally, would happily nurture rows of them in a garden box if only they would stay there. By definition, a weed is just a plant growing someplace you don't want it. But some weeds are especially invasive and grow everywhere you don't want them. Dandelions are one of those. They are extremely aggressive and hardy and quickly spread to choke out every other plant. And once released, they are almost impossible to reign in.

I've successfully tackled highly aggressive and hardy invasive species before with very positive results. Most notably, there was the Scotch Broom Offensive of 1999—after which, of course, we partied; and the Blackberry Bramble Campaign of 2012.

Scotch Broom is an incredible nuisance that someone decided would be nice to transplant from Scotland to Canada, an act akin to having been cured of cancer and then taking up smoking. Broom is an evergreen bush with vibrant yellow blossoms in summer and not an unattractive plant. Like most weeds, it falls into that classification purely by virtue of its lack of restraint. It's a tenacious bush that grows and spreads with amazing speed, quickly choking out all the competition and taking over vast swaths. Once established, it's nearly impossible to kill. The roots are deep and secure, and the plant itself is as tough as leather, fibrous and rubbery, and very difficult to cut.

In 1990 I cleared a substantial tract of forest to make way to build my first house. It took me about three years to complete that project, and when I stepped back to examine my work, I suddenly realized that my house was now set amid a forest of Scotch Broom. I began the landscaping phase of the project by addressing this issue.

At this point, I should mention that I don't like loud things, nor do I like using chemicals. It's not that I'm a rabid environmentalist; it's just my nature. I prefer to do things slowly and quietly and my tools of choice are my mind, my body, patience, and persistence. It drives my wife crazy.

So in addressing Scotch Broom, my first effort was two weeks of sawing and chopping the entire grove to the ground. In the end, I had two huge piles, which I intended to let dry in the scorching summer sun, then burn. I waited and watched expecting the pile of green to blanch then turn brown. It never happened. After a couple of months, the green had darkened and I was surprised that the plants had become even more rubbery and difficult to cut. There was no chance that it would burn. I decided to apply more patience and waited until the next summer. I poured gasoline over a pile and tried to burn it, but the flames only lasted as long as the accelerant. Meanwhile, I had a fresh crop as large as the first.

At that point, I knew I was out of my depth and willing to apply chemicals, a horde of locusts or radiation. I took the radical step of seeking out expert advice and visited a nursery. The man shook his head and sadly told me that though they sold some herbicides that might temporarily relieve the problem, the only method he knew of that would guarantee success, especially over such a large area, was to exhaust the roots by continually cutting the plants to the ground until other plants choked them out.

Far from being discouraged, I was thrilled because this kind of plan perfectly suited my nature. For the next three years, I religiously pulled out seedlings and cut every other bush to ground level, leaving the remains to slowly rot. A forest of fast-growing poplar trees sprouted all around which eventually altered the environment enough for native plants to regain control, and the broom ceased to be a problem. It took a few more years for the forest to recycle those large, old piles.

Years later, I bought my second house. It had been poorly maintained and the yard was entirely overtaken by blackberry bushes. Some of the brambles were almost as thick as my wrist! In my area, this is a very common plant and I was very familiar with its nature; invasive and persistent—like my own, but with gouging brambles, as well.

I elected to apply the same technique as with the Scotch Broom: Exhaust the roots. Knowing that blackberry bushes readily sprout

The name Dandelion refers to the jagged shape of the leaves and comes from the French: "dente de lion" which translates as "lion's teeth."

Interestingly, though, the French call it pissenlit which translates as "urinate in bed," because the plant is a diuretic.

wmdean.com

new shoots from cut off branches, I first hacked them to the ground, piled them and then took the extra precaution of reducing every stalk to 6-inch pieces! I was determined to eradicate this weed in a single pass. I then covered the piles with black plastic to hasten the rotting process and turned my attention to the interior of the house for about two years. During this period, I continued to scan the yard regularly, dispatching anything resembling a blackberry. In the summer, I sprayed the rotting piles with water to keep them moist and feed the decay.

This all worked as expected. I planted grass, which quickly took over, and, after about three years, I no longer had any blackberries.

Around here, broom and blackberries are two of the biggest nuisance plants we have to deal with. Dandelions are the third.

This year, I decided to go for the trifecta.

Having been twice successful, I applied the same technique. Dandelions blossom in spring. It's June now and I regret to report that exhausting the roots is exhausting me!

Dandelions are like icebergs with the majority of the plant hidden below ground. Common wisdom is that the only way to get rid of them is to pull out the entire taproot. The ground around my house is mostly clay: hard as a rock half the year and soft as boot-sucking syrup the rest of the time. Knowing this, I started in February when the ground was still soft and uprooted as many Dandelions as I could: We're talking about hundreds and hundreds of plants. It wasn't easy because, even in the softened clay, the roots often broke while being pulled. There was no hope of getting them all, but I did make a substantial dent. By the time they began to blossom, there were only a few hundred.

My initial idea was simply to pluck every yellow blossom and let the plants waste energy regenerating; hoping the surrounding grass and clover would choke them out. Unfortunately, the clay is a challenge for everything except Dandelions and the grass was slow to take over. By the time the sun started shining regularly, in May, the ground was too hard for new grass to sprout.

Still I kept plucking. It was easy because the bright yellow blossoms were easy to spot. I started by making rounds each morning before setting off to work. When I returned 6 hours later, I was surprised at how many I had missed. Eventually, I realized that what had been a nub in the morning was a blossom by afternoon. I stuck to plucking only blossoms for a time but was soon making three rounds a day. So then I advanced the program to include the buds. This was a little more difficult as they lie lower and are green, making them harder to spot, but I soon became skilled at picking them out.

Then I discovered that many of the blossoms I had plucked and tossed aside had continued to bloom into white puffballs of seed! After that, I began collecting every amputated bud or blossom and disposing of them in the compost pile.

I felt like I was making progress. Passers-by remarked that mine was the only yard in the neighborhood uninfected by Dandelions. Of course, what they didn't know was that I spent an hour each day plucking off the heads.

The spring of 2016 was typically mild, but rainier than usual, so all the plants thrived—including the Dandelions. Mid-April was the peak of the battle and I was growing despondent. The Dandelion numbers did not seem to be decreasing. I went to Phase Three and started pulling off the leaves as well as buds. The grass needed mowing by this time and I thought those would be easier days, as the mower would do my job for me. Turns out, rather than fear my lawn mower, Dandelions seem to regard it as an invigorating massage. A few hours after mowing, there always bloomed a fresh crop of blossoms. The next time I mowed the lawn, I watched more carefully as I passed over and discovered that the heads of the weed were pushed downward by the wind from the lawn mower blade and they often escaped the cutting edge. Nature is an impressive architect!

Phase Four included mowing, then a round of plucking blossoms, buds and leaves and then, for good measure, running a weed eater over the Dandelions, reducing them to ground-level nubs.

In early June, after four months of hard work and constant vigilance, I felt that I could finally rest as the blossoms were now few and far between. It felt like victory until I learned that peak Dandelion season ends in June. It will be eight more months before I know for sure. But it's a foreboding omen that when I pulled aside the black tarp over the compost heap I discovered a thick grove of Dandelions, limp and anaemic, but alive, nonetheless. To be safe, I am slowly transferring these to the trash bin, doing my part to beautify our local landfill.

Dandelions have proved to be my most challenging vegetative adversary, but I can not allow them victory as it sets a bad example to the other weeds and gives my kids another reason to mock me. If next spring finds the Dandelion population blooming I'll be forced to move to Phase Five, and we can all learn to love the smell of Roundup in the morning.

A Girl Named Cheerio-ko

My wife, Junko *(June•koh)*, is horrible at making decisions. Or she's a master. I can't decide.

It wasn't until a month after the birth of our daughter that she could agree on a name. It was a frustrating process for me. Each day, during the pregnancy, I came to her with names I thought were good and she vetoed them all:

Me: What about Laurel? It sounds very poetic.
Junko: I'm Japanese. Nothing with an 'L' or an 'R' in it.
Me: What about Margaret? It sounds smart.
Junko: I'm Japanese. Nothing that ends with a consonant, other than 'N.'
Me: What about Imogen? It sounds sophisticated.
Junko: That means "horse poop" in Japanese. *(It doesn't.)*
Me: What about Stephanie? I think it's drop-dead sexy.
Junko: Wasn't that the name of your ex?

In the meantime, our family referred to our child as Cheerio-ko based on her ahead-of-the-curve accomplishment of having once sucked on a Cheerio.

Me: You've got to decide soon.
Junko: Why? She has no idea that she has no name.

I can see, now, that this was a valid point, but I am panicky by nature and was busy doing what came naturally.

Me: You can't leave her nameless. In all of human history no one without a name has ever accomplished anything worth mentioning.
Junko: You seem agitated.
Me: This shouldn't be so difficult. Even my bologna has a first name.
Junko: Huh? Is this performance art?
Me: The family's calling her Cheerio-ko!
Junko: That's cute.
Me: Are you kidding me? What if that name sticks and she accidentally kills someone. Even if it was in self-defence, she's still going to be labelled a cereal killer.

There are certain etymological advantages to arguing with someone in their second language, but if the word play fooled Junko, she didn't let on.

Junko: Ok, then. How about No-na-mey?

I immediately phoned all of my family members and excitedly announced that a decision had been made. The baby has a name, something Japanese: No-na-mey!

A few hours later, when I wrote it down on paper, the truth leapt off the page at me. "Noname," it turns out, is not a Japanese name; it just sounds like one. When you see it on paper, it is obviously English, and obviously: "No Name." I was chagrined, both at having fallen for it, and at having been so smoothly tricked, in my native language.

A few days later, seemingly out of the ether, Junko came up with the name "Rihana."

By this time I would have said yes to "Horse Poop," in any language. I like "Rihana" but it seems an odd culmination of ten month's worth of ruminating. It is not quite "Rihanna" which would be quickly understood most anywhere in the world, and it seems a somewhat random combination of syllables to all the Canadians and Japanese we meet. Every time we introduce our daughter, the response is an awkward pause followed by the same set of mundane questions: *You mean Rihanna? Is it Japanese/Canadian? What does it mean? Could you spell that again?*

Also: Since when were 'R's' allowed

Junko assures me, it looks amazing when written in Kanji characters.

Thank goodness we didn't have to come up with a last name.

It's usually a good thing, but my wife gets her way, a lot.

Such is the power of *not* wanting.

Approaching deadlines carry little weight with Junko, who often makes her final decision long after most people consider the matter

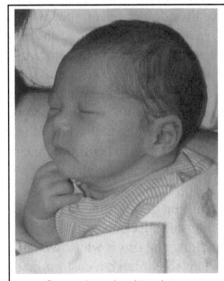

Our newborn daughter sleeps, seemingly unaware that she is nameless.

Six years later, my daughter frolicks, seemingly unconcerned that she was almost nameless.

closed. As you can imagine, this generates a lot of agitation and inconvenience for others. It's stressful for me, as well. I've spent most of my working life responsible for making deadlines. Also, I have a lifelong habit of arriving awkwardly early to house parties. When, exactly, to arrive at events remains one of our most consistent and contentious marital issues.

But I'm experienced now and can look at things from many perspectives. In one light, I see people as walking collections of systems and agendas. And I'm wise enough to know that every system has its advantages. Junko's decision-making process is no exception.

In order to maintain control of a situation, it's easiest if you can let go of the outcome. In other words, if you don't care which way things go, if you are able to walk away from the result, then no one can use your desire to manipulate you. This is particularly true when shopping, and Junko wields this power like a Samurai.

If you are ever shopping in Victoria, Canada and arrive at the cash register to find three store managers and a cashier huddled around a little Asian woman with a cartload of groceries and a fistful of coupons, either move to another line or open a package of Doritos and settle in. Odds are those store managers are going to lose the argument and the longer they fight, the more they'll lose in interrupted sales. And, if by some small chance they do not relent, they will be doing a lot of restocking, because regardless of the fact that she may have spent an hour gathering her groceries, and an hour before that planning the coupons and memorizing store policy, she is absolutely prepared to walk away with all of our money still in her purse. She considers that a relative win, because, ultimately, it's a loss to the store. Either way, that cash register is going to be tied up for a while. Wiser store managers rubber stamp everything and wave her through. Unwise ones drink heavily, after hours—which may, or may not, have anything to do with Junko.

In our consumer-based society, instant gratification has become the expectation, and the power of not wanting can be impressive.

Junko is not quick to decide anything and this is why it was only two weeks prior to our wedding when she ordered a custom made ring through a local specialty jeweller. Our salesman was also the owner; a large, hairy man of about 35, well dressed and draped in gold chains, with rings on most of his fingers. His hair was shiny black and slicked down; his manner, charming and charismatic. He exuded confidence, almost to the point of arrogance, but you got the impression that his faith in himself was not unfounded. After a few rounds of bartering with Junko, he agreed to a lower price and a higher quality ring, custom made to her specifications, guaranteed to arrive from his Vancouver shop in time for the wedding. As the ring had to be purchased sight-unseen, we were assured that, if we were not totally satisfied, we could cancel the order at any time—including after it arrived—and that our deposit would be fully refunded. Myself, feeling the pressure of the looming deadline, I was just happy to finally have the decision made.

With Too-Good-To-Be-True deals, buyers usually hope for the best but prepare for the worst. Whenever a salesman over-promises, most people implicitly understand that there may be compromises and, by the time those compromises arise, are so emotionally locked into the end result that they will bend to accommodate. Our salesman forgot that "most people" does not mean "all people." He knows better, now.

The wedding day drew nearer but, despite assurances, the ring did not appear. About three days before the wedding, Junko returned to with the jeweller. He finally admitted that it did not look like the ring would arrive in time. He then offered to sell us another ring for the wedding day and do an exchange when her ring came.

Junko looked at the salesman, her eyes large and smiling and politely declined his kind offer. When she spoke, her English was, of course, infused with her Japanese accent, but she enunciated each word carefully and clearly, suggesting that, at this point, it might be best to cancel the order and get our deposit back.

He blanched.

And, in that instant it became obvious that he'd known when he sold us the custom ring that it was unlikely to get here in time, but assumed that once he had our money and her heart was set on the design, she would be too emotionally invested, and it would seem too awkward, to ask for a refund—especially knowing that the custom ring was under construction and would be difficult for him to sell to another. He had tried to manipulate her and was about to find out that she had known this all along and been prepared to ignore it, but only so long as things fell her way. The jeweller recovered quickly and offered to lend her a ring for the ceremony. You could tell he thought this a magnanimous offer that could not be refused. She thanked him for his thoughtfulness but declined on the basis that she would rather marry with no ring than with a ring that was not hers. There was a short pause during which the salesman and I absorbed her declaration and tried to imagine a one-ring wedding ceremony.

I thought I knew my wife-to-be, but this was another of those many instances in which I was wrong. It had never occurred to me that she might be perfectly happy to get married without a wedding ring. It had never occurred to the jeweller, either. In this, as in many other ways, she is not your average consumer.

By this time, we were familiar figures to his staff and I could feel them all surreptitiously watching the exchange. Things were getting interesting.

The conversation went a few more lines with him finally implying that she did not trust him to which she replied in the sweetest of tones that although his intentions have been very generous, she had a list of the promises he had made or implied to this point which had not been fulfilled. She listed them. Delicately couching complaints within compliments and with a politeness that bordered on condescension, she went on to explain that, based on these failed promises, the quality and workmanship of the custom-made ring was also in question. This approach seemed to tazer his brain, making it, at once, impossible to refute and impossible for him to take offence.

The jeweller went completely silent and just stood, staring at her. Me too. In fact, the entire shop was stone silent. I think, maybe, street-traffic had come to a halt, as well.

Then, he did something that I'm sure he had never done before. Suddenly, and stiffly he went behind the counter, unlocked a safe, and returned our money to us. He was smiling, but he was not happy. All his employees were staring as if water were being transformed into wine.

As we left, he managed a weak smile and invited us to return; the mark of a true professional, but it was obvious that he did not welcome a rematch.

Had Junko not been there, I would have walked out owning a ring I did not want and, probably, a set of matching earrings. I have never been more impressed. I should have been frightened. I know better, now.

In the end, Junko changed her mind, entirely, and decided she'd rather have a very simple gold band as a wedding ring. We bought one of the cheapest ones we could find in a mall, somewhere.

About a year later, the diamond popped out of Junko's engagement ring and we were forced to replace it, under insurance. To my surprise, she insisted that we return to that same store because they had given us the best deal, on paper. There, she dealt with the same man as if the first incident had never happened. But you could tell that, for him, the emotional scars had not healed, and the fact that the incident seemed to hold no weight with her probably prolonged his recovery. He did not strut as he had before; seemed timid, in fact. Rather than talking to us like old friends, as he had the first time, he remained distant and formal throughout, probably wondering if she were now toying with him; a strange woman who spent idle hours bargaining salesmen into untenable promises, and then shaming them.

To this day, we've never purchased anything from that store.

The power of not wanting extends past the shopping mall. Junko refuses to be rushed, letting go of anything she feels can be used to pressure her.

Three years ago, our mortgage was up for renewal and our long-time banker had recently moved away. Unlike the previous person, the new woman assigned to us was clearly more interested in the bank's welfare than in ours. The deal she offered us was on par with every other institution, but we were used to getting a few extras because of our long association with that bank and our previous banker. Suddenly, I no longer felt "richer than I think I am." I had not expected this and had left the negotiations until close to the expiry of our mortgage. There was no time for shopping around. I took the deal home and talked to Junko about it, told her that we should accept it for now, and use the next five years to shop around. Junko listened but did not say much. A few days later I noticed that she had not signed the documents. When I asked her about it, she told me she was still thinking. I didn't see what there was to think about, we were only a couple of days away from the deadline. I began to panic. I'd never missed a payment or a contract deadline and had no idea what might happen if we didn't sign. I was worried about losing the house, or being forced to accept a lesser deal. I argued with her and became very upset. Finally, I threw up my arms and told her that she could handle the whole thing.

The deadline passed. Turns out, that when the old mortgage lapses, the bank continues to finance the property, but they apply their current standard rates. However, they are aware that you are not locked in and may leave whenever you find another financial institution offering a better deal. A week later, our phone rang. It was the bank, offering us a better deal.

You might wonder what happens when you come up against an adversary who is equally skilled in employing the not wanting system. Well, that occurs daily in our household. It is not nearly as elegant as the above scenarios and often involves tears, shouting and pouting.

And, it's why I think we should have named our daughter Karma.

Three Original Fairy Tales...
Daddy-Style!

My kids are nine- and eleven-years-old, and sometimes when they are especially devious, they appeal to my writer's ego to manipulate me into making up a story at bedtime. Fortunately, their standards are low, and the story doesn't have to be entertaining, as long as it prolongs their evening.

Here is a transcript of this evening's session:

Noah: Dad, tell us a story.
Rihana: Yeah, your stories are the best, Dad!
Noah: Yeah, Dad. The best!
Me: Well…
Both kids: Pleeeeeezzz?
Me: Ok. Once upon a time, there was a little boy named Noah who had a small pet rabbit. He fed it carrots, but it refused to eat. So then he tried cabbage, but again, it did not eat. He tried corn and peas and licorice and coffee and tobacco. But it would not eat any of these things, which, on the whole, was probably for the best as rabbits are jumpy enough. One day, as Noah bent to fill the rabbit's bowl with amphetamines, the creature nipped off a lock of the boy's hair and began to chew greedily. That's when Noah realized that his bunny was actually… a hare.

Both kids: D-a-a-a-d!

They're groaning dramatically and rolling their eyes, but I can tell they liked it.

Me: Ok, ok. Once upon a time, there was a little girl named Rihana who had a small pet fly. Why did she have a pet fly? Because she was *that* poor, that's why. Anyway, she tried feeding her fly fly-foods but it refused to eat. She tried fermented fruit, but it did not eat. She tried rotten vegetables, but it would not eat. She tried raw sewage, but still, her pet fly refused to eat. Finally, one day she was making a butter sandwich (because she was too poor to afford jam) and a small speck of butter flew off of her finger (because she couldn't afford a knife) and onto the lid of her fly's jar. The fly immediately buzzed over to it and started licking the butter through the single air hole (because she was too poor to afford more air holes) and that's when she realized that her fly was actually... a butterfly!
Both kids: D-a-a-a-d! Seriously?

Those simple ideas occurred to me a few weeks ago and I'd held on to them for just such an occasion. But earlier, at dinner, another one popped into my head and I've used those first two stories to stall while I gather and organize the elements for this one...

Me: OK. I will now tell you the tragic tale of The Man with Three Birds...

One day a man walked into a pet shop and purchased a beautiful bird and a beautiful golden cage in which to keep him. The bird had feathers of every color of the rainbow and sang a hundred beautiful songs; many of them Taylor Swift's. The man was very pleased with his purchase and every day he spent hours gazing into the golden cage at the gorgeous creature, listening to its top one hundred
But one day, the bird no longer sang and the man was puzzled. This continued and the man became concerned. He returned to the pet shop and sought advice. The store owner sold him the very best seed after which he immediately returned home and filled the bird's

bowl with the expensive mixture. But this changed nothing. A few days later he returned again to the pet shop and sought more advice. The store owner pondered, and then suggested a mirror. Perhaps if the bird had the image of another bird to sing to, it would restore its inspiration to sing. The man bought a large and ornate mirror that matched the cage and installed it, but this also changed nothing. Once more the man returned to the pet store and this time the owner sold him a golden brush with which to preen the bird, one feather at a time. The man did this for hours, religiously, every day and yet the bird would not sing.

Finally, in desperation, the man gathered up the cage and returned to the pet store whereupon, after hearing his customer's complaint, the manager took one look at the tiny creature and declared, "Well, I know what your problem is."

"You do?" asked the man, hope swelling in his heart.

"Oh yes. Absolutely," said the store owner. "This bird's dead."

So the store owner sold that same man another bird that he guaranteed would sing and was of a much heartier stock so that it was much less likely to stop singing just because of death. The man went home and was thrilled as the bird sang a sad, but beautiful song all the way home and on into the night. But after a few weeks, the man became depressed. The bird would only sing heart-rending melodies that made the soul ache. He thought to cheer the bird by filling its bowl with the highest quality seed that he'd previously purchased for his last pet. Greedily, the bird ate the seed but still its songs remained sad. Then the man thought, perhaps the bird is lonely, so he installed the mirror that he'd purchased for his last bird. The bird spent hours ogling and singing to his reflection, but all the songs remained sad. Finally, the man returned to his ritual of brushing each feather with the special brush he'd purchased at the pet store, but no matter how much time and care he invested, the bird's songs remained sad.

Finally, in desperation, the man gathered up the cage and returned to the pet store whereupon, after hearing his customer's complaint, the manager took one look at the tiny creature and declared, "Well, I know what your problem is."

"You do?" asked the man, hope swelling in his heart.

"Oh yes. Absolutely," said the store owner. "This bird's a blue bird."

At this point, the man became agitated. Feeling that the pet store owner had twice deceived him, he returned the bird and this time he chose his own bird, not allowing the store owner to say a word so that he might not be thrice led astray. Perusing the store, he came upon a magical-seeming creature that could spontaneously alter its colour to any hue of the rainbow. The bird did not sing, but it was so lovely and unusual in form that the man was very pleased, and anyway he now considered the lack of voice to be a blessing. Refusing all help from the store owner, he placed the bird in the cage himself, paid and returned home.

Much to the man's delight this bird's magic did not diminish. It still changed colour many times a day and, blissfully, remained mute. But after about a week, the man noticed that the bird looked thin and frail. He immediately filled its dish with the premium bird seed, but the bird refused to eat and a few days later, looked even thinner. He installed the mirror and though the bird did gaze into it, it continued to weaken until it fell from its perch and lay, listless, at the bottom of the cage. He got the special brush and brushed the bird's entire body, leaving no patch unpreened. But still, the bird continued to deteriorate.

The man was very concerned, but suspecting that he had now been thrice fooled and not keen to endure more humiliation, he did not return to the pet store. Instead, he took the frail creature in his hands and stepped out onto the balcony of his 55th-floor apartment, leaned out over the railing and drew back his hands, setting the little bird free; at which point it plummeted the entire 55 floors, magically transforming into a small red smudge on the sidewalk below.

The man was horrified at what had occurred and immediately called a veterinarian who arrived within minutes whereupon, after hearing his customer's complaint took one look at the remains of the unfortunate creature and declared, "Well, I know what your problem is."

"You do?" asked the man, hope swelling in his heart.

"Oh yes. Absolutely," said the veterinarian. "This is a Chameleon."

Both kids: Goodnight, Dad.
Me: Nailed it!

82

The Family Calendar

Every year—usually around Black Friday, to get the best deal—I log into VistaPrint.com and upload a bunch of the previous year's family photos and create a calendar for the coming year. They always arrive quickly and look great and I order enough copies that I can use them as gifts for those people on my Christmas list whom are particularly hard to buy for. *(Let this be fair warning to those who know me and fail to drop overt hints as to what they might like for Christmas.)*

Even though I live with her every day, my wife is by far the most difficult puzzle on my Christmas list and so she automatically gets one. The first time I did it, it was unexpectedly well received and so, of course, I now repeat the action every year partially because I learn new tricks so quickly and partially because I am so slow to learn new, new tricks. My wife likes it because it's covered in pictures of her family, but also because she finds it useful for keeping track of all the appointments for her and the kids. Whenever I see it hanging on the wall, dates filled with ink, I smile, reflecting on that rare feeling of having bought a gift that turned out to be appropriate.

I try to find photos from the previous year, representing each month and include as much of the entire family as I can, though the four of us are the main feature. I definitely try to avoid anything morbid but feel that to be representative, I must include some negative things. This year's calendar featured a picture from the emergency room after my brother's bicycling accident. It's a headshot of Mike just before getting a huge train track sewn across a wide gash on his left cheek.

I remember when I was taking this picture thinking that his days of being the better-looking brother were over. How good looking is he? Well, a beautiful girl—a complete stranger—once came up to him in a bar, kissed him on the lips and whispered, "I just had to." Where I might have replied something unintelligible weakly followed by, "... call me?" he smiled, said something akin to "I understand," but probably much cooler, then returned to his beer while the rest of us chopped livers watched in stunned silence as she sauntered away in slow motion; long, lustrous hair blowing and backlit. I remember her to this day. He doesn't. Turns out, it wasn't the first time. Nor was it the last.

A few years back, we were in Vegas with a cadre of friends celebrating Mike's 50th birthday. At 50, I assumed that he was past his prime and hanging out with him would be a reasonably safe place for my ego. He and I wanted to see Cirque de Soliel but the tickets were a little more expensive than we'd expected and we hoped to get a deal by waiting until just after the doors closed before purchasing. There wasn't much of a line-up, which either meant that everyone had pre-booked or that there might be some empty seats. My brother offered to watch the theatre doors and then queue up at the last second. Meanwhile, I nursed a drink in a nearby lounge with Patricia, one of our friends who found herself at loose ends because all of our other friends were busy gambling and she'd literally shot her wad the day before firing machine guns, at about twenty cents a bullet.

Patricia: I paid a hundred dollars for five-hundred bullets and stood in line, in the blazing sun, for nearly two hours to learn one interesting fact: An Uzi 9 mm fires 600 bullets a second.

She was interested in seeing Cirque de Soliel but, instead, resigned herself to the cost-saving measure of watching TV in her room for a couple of hours until we all regrouped for dinner.

When the doors closed, there was no line-up at the ticket booth. But seconds before my brother stepped up to the booth, a man approached him offering a free ticket. Apparently, he'd been stood up and as the doors were closing, the ticket would otherwise go to waste. My brother hesitantly accepted the gift, then proceeded forward and bought two more tickets for the show at a very-last-minute-discount of twenty percent—better than we'd hoped. Mike then re-gifted that free ticket to Patricia.

Only about two-thirds of the seats were occupied but being good Canadians, we all stuck with the seat numbers on our tickets, though that put us quite a distance apart.

If you've never seen Cirque de Soleil I wholeheartedly recommend it, though I cannot adequately describe it. All I can say is, forget what you know of circus and theatre and prepare yourself for two hours of a breathtaking, heart-stopping performance during which your only two thoughts will be: "Oh my God! That's absolutely gorgeous!" and "Oh my God! Any second now, someone's going to die!"

No one died.

Afterward, our little threesome reconvened in the lobby and Patricia told us what had happened immediately after she took her seat…

Stranger: [in the seat next to her] Excuse me, but you're in my seat.
Patricia: Excuse me? What?
Stranger: I purchased that seat for my friend.
Patricia: [examining her ticket] My ticket shows this number.
Stranger [and stranger]: Hey! I gave that ticket to a man.
Patricia: And he gave it to me.
Stranger: [clearly agitated] Well, it wasn't for you. It was for him!

After which he loudly *harumpfed!*, slumped deeply into his seat, arms tightly crossed, and sat making seething sounds, like the fuse of a large firework.

Patricia moved to an empty seat and enjoyed the show.

The free ticket had been part of a very clever—though flawed—pick-up manoeuvre. Had it worked, my brother would have ended up sitting next to the man, who we now understood was gay, giving him an opportunity to flirt with Mike. There's no denying that a man's good looking when his attractiveness is so extreme that it transcends gender!

To my chagrin, a few months after the ER, Mike's uncanny X-man-like healing powers left him with a faint, almost decorative scar which served no more purpose than to transform his boyish good looks into rakish good looks. If I didn't love him, I'd hate him.

Meanwhile, back at the calendar: My wife wants the kids to take a multivitamin every day. They do it on their own, but as a check, she asks them to make a mark on the calendar if they have taken their daily dose. Last year, I noticed that between her appointments and the kids' vitamin marks, the day-squares became very crowded. And, one time, I heard her complain that there was not enough space to pencil in a new event.

So, this year, I ordered a much larger calendar. As usual, it was a welcomed gift—for my wife, if not my six-year-old niece. Her own fault, really, for putting only "drone" on her Christmas list.

Today, twenty-eight days into the new year, I glanced at the calendar expecting to see some squares neatly filled in with events and appointments. The picture below shows what I saw.

Apparently, the kids assumed the extra space was meant entirely for them. A sound assumption, as most everything else is. The simple act of signing off on their vitamin has escalated into some sort of graffiti war and the entire spaces are now occupied territory.

I immediately ran to tell my wife. Sometimes a husband needs attention, too. She said, "It's cute."

Cute? I once got reamed out for putting a smiley face in the corner, on her birthday: "It looks constipated. I thought you were mad at me. If you have to scribble, please do it on your own birthday."

Sometimes, Life can be unfair.

So far, this year, my obsessively punctual wife has missed three appointments.

And, sometimes, Life evens things up a bit.

Gifting Grievances

I'm that person who has everything. I've noticed that there are a lot of ads depicting gifts for me. These are lies. You know what that "person who has everything" really wants? By definition: Nothing.

I know that I'm impossible to buy for and I wish my family would stop trying.

I don't actually have everything, but I am very satisfied with what I do have and can afford to buy anything I need, and most everything I want. Those few things that I can not afford are beyond the budget of anyone else I know. Also, I've been told that I am very picky. I prefer to call it "discriminating," which, I suppose, pretty much proves that point.

I don't try to be difficult, but I'm a middle class, North American adult and if I really want something, I buy it. Therefore, if I didn't buy it I didn't want it. I've told my family this, repeatedly. And yet they persist. One Christmas, I even posted the concept on social media. Surprisingly, it did not go viral.

Birthday and Christmas gifts are appropriate for children, as they generally don't have the means to purchase every single thing that they want or need. But with manufacturers cheaply churning out millions of copies of every possible thing while online marketers make them irresistibly accessible, it's hard for parents not to spoil their offspring. Whether your kid is into Lego, Superheroes, Harry Potter, Barbie or vintage Elvis bobbleheads *(you know your kid's not like other kids, right?)* you can find it and you can probably afford to purchase it. Worse yet, your child knows this.

To combat this, my wife and I err on the side of giving too little, as opposed to too much. This has made our children unusually easy to please but still failed to solve the problem. Paradoxically, because of their minimal expectations, a day rarely goes by where they don't have a stocking-stuffer moment. My son is a Pokémon freak. Give him a single sticker and his eyes light up and he vibrates like a lab rat on sugar-coated Cocaine. Similarly, if you present my daughter with a printed out Harry Potter coloring sheet, she will tear up and hug you until it gets awkward. They are aged eleven and nine. It may be relevant to point out that they are home schooled. With the bar set so low, it's difficult to stem the flow of what they consider to be gifts. So, for them, every day is mini-Christmas.

Their friends have similar experiences but on a grander scale. Those few things that the average kid lacks are beyond our gift-giving budget. I suspect that's why a trend amongst our circle of parents is to limit birthday gifting. A typical invite may mention a token monetary donation—usually for charity—but will clearly state "no gifts." The pendulum has swung so far that each party guest receives a complimentary "goody bag," just for showing up. I'm not sure why there have to be goody bags. Why can't humans be happy with a zero-sum game? I wish that we could all just agree that none of us really needs anything and that celebrations are best when they are about getting together rather than getting presents?

At least kids love receiving gifts. For me, unwanted items are a burden. I resent having to store, organize and redistribute them. Most are re-gifted, donated, or sold.

If you are ever in my neighborhood, you'll want to make a point of checking out my summer garage sale: We are always overstocked, and everything is priced to sell! It's all about divestment. Price is merely a formality and almost everything is brand new. Beyond un-treasured gifts, you will also find a year's worth of my wife's excess couponing purchases—things we don't use but that she made money on, by buying. It's all name brand and typically includes candy, shaving cream, shampoo, hair dye, electronic soap dispensers, scented candles and cleaning products.

My extended family makes a point of visiting my garage sale, though they never buy anything. They come to find out whether I really appreciated the gift they gave me, six months previous. I see it as a classic demonstration of "if you ask for it, the Universe will deliver." My family really, really asks for it—assuming, of course, by "it" you mean disappointment. Consequently, I endure a family rep for being cold and unsentimental, and am sometimes lovingly referred to as "The Grinch Who Sold Christmas." In silent retaliation, I've labeled them all "slow learners."

I've told them my feelings. I've demonstrated my resolve. And yet, each Christmas or birthday I still get saddled with gifts for the guy who has everything—a stylish ornament which never matches our "day-care chic" decor, an animated plastic object that sings an irritating song the entire time you're desperately trying to gouge out the batteries, or another pocket knife. I'd still have more knives than pockets even if I wore cargo pants, a fishing vest, trench coat and a billiard table. I've used a pocket knife exactly once in my adult life— to pry open another pocket knife for someone at my garage sale. On balance, I probably don't whittle as often as I should.

If I wanted bad gifts, I would just keep all those art projects my kids bring me to decorate my office. Ok, maybe I am a little bit cold. But, to be fair, my kids have far too much free time and are very industrious.

Well, At Least They Tried:

One Christmas, my family thought it would be a good idea if, instead of stressing out to buy a couple of dozen gifts, we put our names in a hat and selected a single person to buy for. Naturally, I was enthusiastic. I drew a name and had an entirely stress-free season—right up until Christmas morning.

There was an unforeseen downside to the name-in-a-hat strategy: it upped the budget, which put additional pressure on that one gift. Instead of gifts valued in the tens of dollars, most people decided that they had to spend hundreds. But anything that expensive really needed to be something the recipient would truly appreciate. By this time I had a policy of only purchasing consumables (i.e. food, engine oil, printer toner) or experiences (i.e. movie passes, elocution lessons, interventions) so this worked well for me. I gave my sister an anger management course, which, as it happened, was not well received. Fortunately, her rant only increased my confidence in the appropriateness of the gift. But it turned out that others had less confidence in their purchases and so, had hedged their bet.

I received a second gift. Followed by a third. Then, a fourth; ending up with just as many unwelcomed gifts as I'd gotten the year before. Apparently, no one else had adhered to the single gift restriction. In secret, they had all reverted to their usual Christmas shopping.

To fill one of the awkward silences, I explained that from my point of view, I was the only one who did not have a "shopping problem." Their counterargument: "Grinch!'

The family never again attempted to tamper with the gift-giving tradition.

As we've grown older, the others are slowly coming around. Gifting the adults has not ended, but it's deescalated into a strange, circular ceremony wherein we all exchange lottery tickets. To me, this is a good idea because millions of dollars happens to be on the short list of things I actually want. However, I'd prefer if we each just bought ourselves a ticket and dispensed with the ceremony, which is as redundant as me buying your kid's Soccer raffle tickets when you buy my kid's Girl Guide cookies. Also, I'm not sure how I'll handle the resentment if my sister wins ten million from a ticket I bought and was forced to give to her in exchange for a losing one.

Gifting The Spouse:

My largest gift-giving problem each year is my wife, Junko. (June•koh)

I see no reason to buy gifts for other adults, but I always want to get something for her in spite of the fact that she's Japanese and this adult gifting idea is completely foreign and somewhat repulsive to her.

Even before she got into couponing, buying a gift for Junko was not easy. She has that traditional Japanese sense of romance which, in case you weren't aware, is just slightly more subdued than a sedated

Vulcan's. Chocolate and flowers are meaningless to her—she does like diamonds, but I feel it's mostly for their economic value and, after fourteen years, we've pretty much exhausted the affordable variations on that theme. And, she's eminently practical, with a hair trigger for returning anything that isn't. This is why I strive to be handy around the house.

On top of all of this, she's a minimalist, rarely purchasing anything extraneous.

In desperation, I now keep a list on my cell phone of anything that she's running low on, or expresses the slightest interest in. This is how a bag of corn starch ended up in her stocking, one year. Things that break can be a source of great joy for me, but I have to balance this against my need to appear handy.

Early on in our relationship, it was established that Junko would always be our household's primary purchasing agent...

Me: What are you talking about? I'm great with money!
Junko: Perhaps. But you are not so great, without money.
Me: . . .
Junko: And, you tend to run out of it very quickly. So, I think it
would be best if I did all the shopping.

The Japanese have a much more complex, yet equally illogical, gift-giving culture which, oddly, Junko thinks makes perfect sense and participates in, to the point of obsession—as is the Japanese way. As in North America, generous gifts are expected for all major events like weddings, birthdays, new year's day and bar mitzvahs. But, as well, there is a huge industry built around exchanging unappetizing confections wrapped in decorative packages to celebrate almost any event...

-"Hello, thanks for coming. Have a cookie."
-"Oh, well thanks for having me. Here's a cookie."

-"Goodbye. Thanks for leaving. Take a cookie."
-"Well, thank you for kicking me out. Please enjoy this cookie."

-"I've been sleeping with your wife. I'm sorry. Please accept this cookie."
-"Thank you for your honesty. Did you get the cookie I left under the pillow?"

-"I accidentally used your toothbrush. Cookie?"
-"Though you are the cable guy and your timing is unusual, it is good that you brushed your teeth. Please, have one of my cookies."
-"Actually, I used it to clean the seat before I used your toilet. Please accept this cookie."
-"Er... you have saved me the trouble of cleaning the toilet seat. Please enjoy a cookie."
-"Actually, my aim was not good. You'd better take the whole box."

Bested. And in my own language. Again!

So, while she doesn't endorse the adult gift-giving idea, she nevertheless participates by acquiring almost all of the gifts we give. And, she does it in her own very special way because she's a couponer. I used to have to be forced to admit this—under my breath, with my head lowered. But now, having seen the thousands of dollars she saves us, each year, I announce it proudly, without prompting—sometimes, without apparent relevance.

When it comes to paying attention to detail, efficiency and innovation, the Japanese are unrivalled. In this regard, Junko makes the rest of her countrymen look like slackers. She spends hours researching and strategizing special offers, rebates, in-store specials and coupons until she's certain to save more than she spends. She not only surpasses the highest shopping and saving standards, she one-ups us native North Americans at our own game because if it's the thought that counts, her gifts are among the most valuable ever given.

We enjoy many other perks from Junko's constant scrimping and saving: a constant stream of rebate checks, free movie tickets, a wide variety of toilet paper, a junk food cupboard that is always full—a junk food cupboard! And, of course, we save money.

But there are unexpected consequences, as well: We don't necessarily get the brand of Peanut Butter we grew up with, we are encouraged to use only a small portion of a single paper towel, we use clothing remnants instead of cloth napkins at the dinner table, depending upon the specials in the produce aisle we may be eating a wide assortment of zucchini and eggplant dishes for a few weeks, and we never get Pop Tarts. And also, she is incredibly difficult to buy for because...

- She shops almost every day and knows all the prices. I must be prepared to defend every purchase.
- She's very conscious of the total amount spent and as the price rises so does her blood pressure. Followed by mine.
- If my gift passes all the other tests, I must still be prepared to hear that she has a coupon for that item and will not be satisfied until I return it, then re-purchase it with the coupon.
- For it to truly be a gift, I must include a trip back to the store to return it. Bought it online and already unboxed it? Well, not only

can she get that precision-packed item back into its original box but, if we're paying the shipping, she'll demonstrate to the manufacturer how it could be safely packed into something smaller.

Last Christmas, the only gifts of mine that she did not ask me to return were a spatula I put in her stocking and cute little gift certificates I made for free massages—which she never redeemed, presumably because she knows exactly how long a free massage lasts and where it leads. I considered it a win.

This Christmas, I lucked out and found a great book that I know she really could use. It cost a hundred dollars and is non-returnable, but I feel confident. It's called, "How to Argue Logically, for Dummies."

This is going to be the best Christmas ever!

17

Adding
Years
to
Your
Age

For most of my life, people have been surprised when they discovered my age, thinking that I am about ten years younger. I can still surprise people, but now that ten-year genetic gift no longer makes me look young, just less old. I have to admit that my body, which I've always considered a temple even if I never treated it that way, could use a new coat of paint and few new shingles. But, even before pretty young girls started calling me "Sir," I was old in the eyes of Western Medicine.

Physical signs that you are dying start sooner and come on quicker than you might expect. For most of us, it's a shock, and is a bit frightening, not to mention embarrassing. But, while you may struggle, Western Medicine is comfortably resigned to the debilitating affects of your old age. Though your condition is both chronic and terminal, it's a less troublesome time, from your doctor's point of view because for every finicky complaint there is a simple diagnosis: old.

That first "old" diagnosis is an "I-told-you-so" moment for those entrenched in Western Medicine which has had it's eagle-eyes on you for quite some time, while perched above ready to swoop down and offer hundreds of chemical remedies.

For me, the first signs of wear began suddenly, at the age of forty. One day I woke up without the ability to read the tiny printed instructions on things I'd purchased at the hardware store. For a time, I got along just assuming everything was dangerous. I bought dollar store magnifying glasses. So long as I never carried a pair with me, I felt that meant that my eyesight was still 20/20-ish. Eventually, I had surrounded myself with magnifiers; stuffed between couch cushions, on top of the toilet paper roll, on shelves, on tables, in cupboards, drawers, and even on top of the fridge. If my desk lamp had been halogen, turning it on might have set the whole place on fire. When I started stacking pairs on top of one another and had run out of nose, I decided it was time to visit an optometrist.

"Why is this happening to me?" I asked.

The young doctor chuckled and offered this detailed explanation: "Your eyes are more than forty years old," in a tone the exact opposite of the one used when evaluating a bottle of fine Scotch. I was tempted to point out that the pyramids still stand and they are more than 4000 years old, but somehow, the fact that I am younger than many buildings did not seem like a powerful argument. Also working against me was the fact that pyramids are often referred to as "ancient" and "ruins."

Me: "Are there some exercises I could do?"

Optometrist: "Many." [waits for my eyes to light up with hope, then adds] "Your abysmal eyesight should not affect your ability to exercise."

Me: [resisting an urge to send him straight to bed without supper] I mean, is there something I can do to improve my eyesight?

Young Whipper-Snapper: Of course. Fill this prescription for glasses.

Naturally, I did what any smart consumer would do when unsatisfied with a medical diagnosis. I got a second opinion. I'm sure that Google would have steered me right, but back then, there was only Yahoo. Based on Yahoo's opinion, I bought a book and a juicer. I drank lots of fresh carrot juice and did eye exercises. The exercises gave me headaches. From the carrot juice I gained a coppery glow and diarrhea. Also, a distaste for carrots—and juicers.

The fact that he was right did not make the young optometrist's advice any more amusing or agreeable. I pegged him at about twenty-five, at that time, and it heartens me to know that he has now reached forty, himself. I finally understand the old adage that revenge is a dish best served cold. It's because it takes so long to prepare.

I give blood regularly and, before every donation, they measure blood pressure. Over the years, I watched the readings climb until, when I was forty-five, it got so high that I could no longer donate. I guess I was like a massively over inflated balloon and they were afraid to prick me with a needle. I consulted a doctor.

"My blood pressure is high," I said.
"You have High Blood Pressure," he declared, putting capital letters on the words to make it official.
"What can I do about it?" I asked.
Doctor: "Take this pill for the rest of your life."
Me: "What if I don't?"
Doctor: "Then your blood will continue pounding away at your internal organs and arteries until something bursts and you spend the rest of your life on dialysis, or dead."

A diagnosis of high blood pressure should not be taken with a grain of salt. I went straight home, delicately lay myself down on the sofa as if an aneurysm bomb were strapped to the base of my brain, and thought about spending the rest of my life dead.

It seemed odd to me that my doctor had never suggested a change of diet, or exercise. I'll bet that when he first started his practice, diet and exercise was always his first advice. But, after thirty years attending patients who would rather take a pill than change their habits, he has become resigned to that fact, and no longer wastes time dispensing good, unheeded advice.

I did a lot of reading on blood pressure and learned that about the only thing that has been shown to reduce it is a low-salt diet. I joined a gym in hopes that an increase in activity might compensate for the fact that the last thing on earth I wanted to lower was the salt in my diet. Three years later, I was in a lot better shape, but none of this had affected my blood pressure.

Eventually, I realized how silly it was of me to resist popping a few grains of a chemical tested and approved by medical professionals when I would happily chug twelve ounces of soda pop on the basis that, though well known to be poison, it's relatively slow-acting and tasty. Reluctantly I filled my first til-death-do-us-part prescription. There can be no greater tribute to my love of salt.

Nothing yells "decrepit!" like sustaining injuries through sleep. When I was about fifty, I awoke one morning with back spasms so painful that I was near tears. The doctor gave me a couple of pills for the short term and comforted me with the assurance that, though there was nothing she could do for me, many people my age live productive lives in chronic pain.

This is what Western Medicine thinks is normal, for a fifty-year-old.

I am a very typical patient in that when I have a complaint large enough to warrant a visit to a doctor, it always turns out that I'm not actually on Death's door, no matter what I saw on the Internet and it's something completely mundane, with solutions that are simple and right out of the textbooks. But, I am *atypical* in that one of my core beliefs is that

Soda Can by Alessandro Paiva,
courtesy of RGBStock.com

exercise is required to maintain health and I am completely willing to exercise in order to avoid or repair injuries and debilitating symptoms, like chronic pain. I assume that this is so atypical that experienced doctors simply skip even hinting at a fitness regime.

For my birthday, my wife had given me a coupon for a massage and now seemed like a good time to redeem it. I went in hoping for a bit of relief and distraction, possibly at the hands of a winsome young girl who might light candles, put on soft music and gently kneed my body with her slender fingers, until my muscles turned to jelly, and pain became the last thing on my mind. When the receptionist showed me to the massage room and mentioned that "Greg" would soon arrive for my session, I clung to a thin strand of hope that she was an exchange student, and that "Greg" was a common female name in Sweden or Thailand.

Alas, Greg was a broad shouldered, strapping young man. But he quickly won me over. He began by asking me if I had any physical issues. I told him about my aching back. Being young, enthusiastic and not yet cynical, he spent more than an hour, examining and testing my musculature, flexibility and range of motion. Afterward, he did a couple of excruciating things which either relieved the pain I was currently experiencing or distracted me from that with new pain. He sent me home with a short list of exercises that he felt would hasten my recovery.

I did those exercises and was soon back to normal, which is abnormal, in the eyes of Western Medicine. The back injury was frighteningly painful and debilitating, so as further insurance, I increased my visits to the gym. Many years later, I am pain free and in better shape.

The most startling and disappointing sign of aging I've experienced is brittle teeth. The first time a tooth broke without reasonable cause, I hadn't had a cavity in more than thirty years. It's scary not being able to depend on parts you've always considered to be in prime condition.

My dentist is cool. He's ok with my calling him Dr. Z because I can't pronounce his last name—also, secretly, it makes me feel James Bond-ish which helps me to squeal in lower octaves, while he pokes my gums with dull needles. Dr. Z is one of those jovial, easy-going guys you can talk to; like a golfing buddy who has erected a tent in your mouth.

Dr. Z: What were you chewing on when this happened?
Me: Hewk.
Dr. Z: Soup, huh. Well, welcome to your senior years.

Diagnosis: old.

Dr. Z: "You might consider switching to astronaut food.

Prescription: perseverance.

Me: ???
Dr. Z: Just kidding. You're not quite there yet. We'll get you back up and masticating, in no time.

I don't believe that my age has much to do with my failing teeth. Because of all the fillings I received when I was a kid, my molars are, basically, thirty-year-old metal with a thin veneer of natural enamel. The good news is that modern porcelain fillings are stronger than those old metal ones and look more natural. With each visit, my teeth grow stronger and my smile, more beautiful.

In the eyes of medical professionals, it seems, the primary cause of everything that goes wrong after the age of forty is having lived past the age of forty. And, to shore up this conviction, they prescribe noxious ointments that smell like decay, just in case you hadn't yet clued in that growing old stinks.

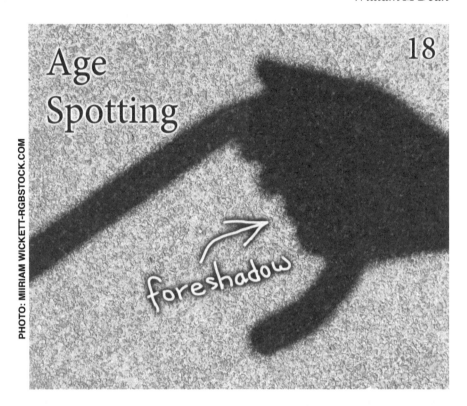

Age Spotting

18

foreshadow

I have tried, but am no longer able to contain the secret that I am aging and, might possibly, already be old. The signs, so far, are small; ranging from slight inconveniences to minor annoyances, but they are reminders that I have reached the point where taking care of myself, no longer takes care of itself.

If I were a banana, I'd be one approaching that border between ripe and rank. Soon, my skin would be speckled and you'd be able to smell me from several feet away. A few age spots and a little A535, and I will be that banana. And, life as an old banana is not grand. First, no one wants to peel you. Then no one even wants to touch you, except the fruit flies—so many fruit flies. Ok, this metaphor may have outlived its usefulness.

For the benefit of those who suspect that they, too, might have become old, I will list some of the subtle signs that I have noticed along the way. If you find yourself relating to any of these points, then best put all your affairs in order—if you're having affairs—and prepare yourself for a new phase in life.

Physiological signs:

- Three factions are fighting it out over turf, on the top of my head: Live hairs, dead hairs and absent hairs.
- My sex drive has diminished enough that I can now tell the difference between love and lust, but not yet so much that I can be counted on to care.
- Apparently, sleep has become a contact sport because I can wake up with aches and pains that did not exist when I went to bed.
- My feet no longer tolerate thin-soled shoes without making my leg bones ache.
- My cast iron stomach is turning to crepe paper.
- Occasionally, and seemingly without reason, my elbows get dry and slightly itchy. When they do, I use my wife's skin cream, which my kids call "Granny Cream" because it smells like little old lady. Perhaps strangers assume that I'm a little old cross dresser.
- Last summer, I got a small itchy patch of dandruff. Instead of buying a whole bottle of Head & Shoulders, I put "Granny Cream" on it and walked around for three days with a greasy splotch of hair that smelled like little old lady and clashed with my cologne. When I was younger, I'd suffer most any inconvenience to try to fit in. Now that threshold is much lower because I'm starting to not care what people think. Also, I'm convinced that no one is watching.
- A hangover is now a guaranteed outcome, lasts two days and can be brought on by a wine gum.
- The only room I can walk into without forgetting why I came is the bathroom.
- I used to pee in the time it takes to slice bread. Now, I could make toast. At some point, I suppose, I'll be able to cook a turkey. That will be convenient, twice a year.
- On Friday nights, I'm in fuzzy slippers and pajamas by eight, and hit the pillow at about the time younger people are hitting the streets.
- People no longer tell me that I look young for my age. Even though I try to stay in shape, the best I get is surprise that I don't look older.
- My ability to shut down at bedtime has also suffered and now I sometimes spend hours staring at the ceiling, worrying about

getting to sleep. There's a crack up there that I should really fix, but then, I think, "What will I stare at?"

- I am writing this article on aging.
- If I put my hand over my heart during the national anthem, people around me become concerned.

- I could still fit all the necessary candles on one birthday cake, but would have to disconnect the smoke alarm. Also, I'd need to buy a larger oven.
- Unless I'm with my parents, wherever I go, I'm the oldest one in the room. Makes me want to go out with my parents more but I want them to drop me off a block early so that no one thinks I'm *with* them. I may be growing older, but no one can force me to mature.
- My father's opinions have started making sense to me. I have developed my own weird opinions, and I know they're weird and yet I nurture these lines of thought hoping they will blossom into precious but smelly flowers, with sharp thorns and poisonous laser beams. I'm becoming cantankerous, and enjoying the process.

Chronological signs:
- I remember when nature was not just a cable channel, and fruit had a season.
- I learned to read and write in cursive.
- My parents smoked in the car with all the windows rolled up while my siblings and I bounced around loose, in the back.
- At the beach, they slathered us in baby oil for a crisp-all-over tan.
- No one has ever seriously called me "Dude."
- Some of the cool words we used when I was a kid: "keen," "far out," "mint," "radical," and "wicked."
- I am psychically separate from my cell phone for hours, each day and, as long as it still works, I don't care that it's not the latest model.
- I know that it's cooler that my cell phone does not flip, but I secretly wish it would, like Captain Kirk's.
- Foods like glazed donuts and vanilla ice cream taste nothing like I remember them, from my childhood.

- My Mr. Miyagi is Pat Morita.
- I still remember all of the actors from movies and TV of my youth, but mostly because their names come up a lot, in obituaries.
- I have partied like it was 1999, because it *was* 1999.
- I once made a girlfriend a mixed tape—on tape.
- When I was young, a package could be shipped, without being handled.
- Mine was the generation that stopped all those VCR's and DVD players from flashing "12:00."

Trying to keep up:
- Because I have kids, I know about Pikachu, but am bewildered that there are 717 others, more than 800 episodes, 20 feature films and thousands of toys. When I was a kid, they were somehow able to produce a toy without making a movie and vice-versa.
- I still appreciate a lot of contemporary music, but have no clue what half the rappers are saying. And, when did "hellagood" become a word?
- I recycle, though I really just want to throw everything into a big pile and burn it, using some Styrofoam as starter.
- I know that Miley Cyrus is no longer a Mousekateer and I'm guessing she doesn't use the word, "Golly," too much anymore.
- I know the terms "selfie," "photobomb," "sexting," "ROTFL," and "twerking." And, because I do a lot of renovations myself, I know what an "epic fail" looks like. But I am still a little fuzzy on "Dubstep."
- I have switched from "Rad!" to "Awesome!"
- I realize that "Sharknado" and "Fifty Shades of Grey" are both popular examples in the modern disaster story genre, I just can't remember which of the two took itself seriously.
- I know that you're not supposed to admit that you like Nickleback. But, I do.
- It's now obvious just how badly I missed the boat on Apple and Google stock and I am resigned to the fact that I am unlikely to see any return on my AOL and MySpace investments.
- I use social media more than most and know more about it than younger people, because I am an independently published author,

and it's part of the marketing side of the job. But, I don't use it to be social.

There are signs yet to come. My mother told me that the first time she felt old was when she walked in on someone who was in the middle of telling a dirty joke, and suddenly, the room went awkwardly silent. If that has happened to you, then you may not be old, but obviously some people think you are. This has not quite happened to me, but the day is drawing near. I've had people at work automatically skip over showing me a picture from Facebook because they assumed I wouldn't really "get it." They're probably right. More telling, yet: I don't care.

The cat is out of the bag and the best I can do now is try to accept it calmly and try to figure out what aging gracefully looks like. I'm told that as compensation for growing old, there is wisdom. And I look forward to that, when it finally arrives. Also, respect, which I understand may come shortly thereafter. But, from where I'm sitting, this seems about as much compensation as a winning touchdown is to the pig.

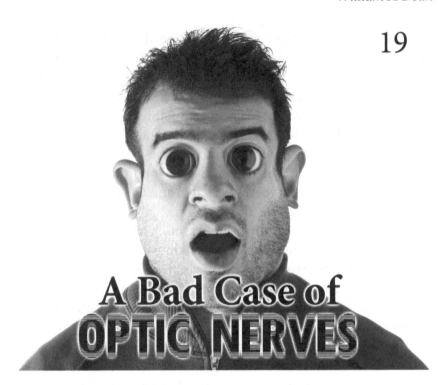

A Bad Case of
OPTIC NERVES

At forty, I lost my vision.

Not all of it, just the most convenient portion that didn't require a mechanical aid sitting on the bridge of my nose every waking second of the day. And my vision is growing steadily worse, so that if there were a disaster tomorrow I'd be scrabbling through the wreckage squinting like a mole person through a shard of broken glass, desperately trying to differentiate between a can of Spam and Friskies.

My mother once told me that the first sign she had of getting old was walking into a room and not remembering why she'd gone there. This started happening to her at the age of forty. Me too. But that never bothered me. I'm not concerned about losing my mind. After all, that's really more of a problem for those around me. Also, it doesn't show. I could lose my entire mind and still look good at a party. But, regardless of my appearance, I wouldn't know therefore I wouldn't care.

For me, the second sign of my aging—the deterioration of my eyesight—had a far larger impact than the first.

It seemed to happen overnight. One day I could pick out individual grains in an hourglass from fifty feet, and the next I had to squint to read an error message with my nose rubbing against the computer screen—doubly disturbing because "error message" was about the only software that really ran smoothly on my old computer.

I figuratively ran to the Internet and literally searched for help. After ruling out aneurysms and brain tumors I stumbled upon the book, "Better Eyesight Without Glasses." Good title—like "Weight Loss by Eating What You've Always Eaten and Doing Less" or "Learn Lithuanian While Watching The Simpsons."

Amazon shipped and, for some reason, handled my book and I had it in hand within the week, by which time I'd already had to make a trip to a dollar store to buy pair of magnifier glasses. I sneaked them into the house in a plain brown paper bag. The irony that I needed glasses in order to read "Better Eyesight Without Glasses" did not escape me.

When I received the book and flipped the front cover, I learned that it was a reprint from a text originally written in 1940. I charged through the first few chapters and was disappointed. Besides being pedantic and obtuse, it was seriously out of date with the exception of the one fact that we all still have eyes. The basic premise seemed to be that I was not actually losing my sight; that I had forgotten how to look. I redoubled my looking, but still failed to see what I was looking at. Still, I was willing to believe, and continued with the suggested exercises. I gave up after chapter seven because I still needed the dollar-store glasses to read the declaration that my vision was "already substantially improved."

I visited an optometrist. I had no intention of submissively slipping on a pair of bifocals; I wanted to know why this was happening and work out some sort of modern eye exercise regime to counter the effect. The optometrist was about twenty-five years old, busy and impatient. Even with my defective eyes I could see that he did not consider himself in the business of answering questions.

"Your eyes are forty years old," he said as if that explained everything; as if nothing in this universe could be expected to function that long? And before I could mention Stone Henge, he slipped corrective lenses before my eyes and gave me a pop quiz.

"Better or worse?" Flipped a gadget and another set of lenses fell in to place.

"Better or worse?" A hundred times in the space of two minutes.

"Better or worse?" It was nerve wracking. Often, I stalled for time, and once or twice I mixed up the two words. I think he scaled the marks.

Then he hastily scribbled a prescription on a scrap of paper. "Next!"

I never filled that prescription.

Three years later, I was still using dollar-store glasses. Of course by then I'd got three pairs; different strengths for different circumstances. There were my TV-specs, book-specs and pill-bottle-specs. You've got to admit, I'm a fighter. The word "stubborn" also comes to mind. Also "denial," and perhaps "foolish." I'm hoping it all averages out to "eccentric."

For months, I was certain that I could exercise my eyes back into shape. But then, one day, my wife said that I was being stubborn, that I couldn't see the forest for the trees and I retorted, "I thought that was a puppy." Clearly, I had run out of salient arguments.

She urged me to stop fighting the physical changes and accept them as a natural by-product of aging.

"Let's see how she feels when she's no longer ten years younger than me," I thought. I said, "But glasses are ugly."

"Better to be looking good than good looking," she replied in her second language.

"Hey! Who's the native English-speaking writer here?" I thought. I said, "Yes, dear."

I don't mind aging—I didn't put up much of a fuss when I went from twenty-two to twenty-three.

I don't mind aging.

What I do mind is growing old.

Glossary of Over-40 Optometric Terms:

- **Optic Nerves:** The disquieting feeling that your vision is failing and you might have to visit an optometrist.
- **Lens Flare:** Irrational rage at your own long-abused body for wearing out and leaving you no option but to visit an optometrist who is barely old enough to shave.
- **Legally Blind:** What is spelled out in large block letters on the eye chart in the optometrist's waiting room. Before you had your glasses, you thought it was a landscape painting but you were $400 richer. Now you begin to wonder if you are losing your sense of humor, as well.
- **Unsightly:** Coke bottle lenses in tortoise-shell frames.

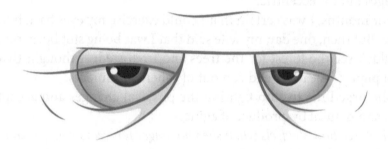

20

A Writer's Mind...

Earlier tonight, I sat down to write an article on human behavior and how we all advertise to each other in subtle ways. But then I started thinking about how I started thinking about that topic, and how much I live in my own mind.

This led to memories of a bad breakup in which my own mind kind of turned on me. From here I remembered Rose, a customer of mine who I wanted to ask out but didn't, and how broken my mind and soul were at the time, and how it was probably best I didn't ask; and, anyway, I think there was a distinct possibility that she would have said no.

I was about forty at the time, and eventually, all the psychic turmoil made me realize that certain aspects of my character needed an overhaul and that it was past time that I started "giving back" to society. So I began donating blood and sponsored an African child, through World Vision. Since then, I have saved countless lives with my sixty-plus pints of AB Negative, and now sponsor two children and also help improve life for eighteen poor families in the Philippines. There are statues of me in the park in my mind, but there's also a lot of pigeon poop. Mostly, cats hang out there. I'm not a big fan of cats.

That dark period also made me realize that living entirely within my own brain was not balanced and that I needed a way to shut off my mind, from time to time. I started going to the gym. A couple of regulars have commented how hard I workout and each time I thought, "That's so true. You'd think I'd be in better shape. If I had worked this hard when I was thirty, I'd look like The Terminator but instead, because I'm now in my mid-forties, I look like Arnold Schwarzenegger... twenty years from now." But I can't say all of that because I'm too busy gasping for air, so I simply grimace and say, "I just make it look hard." The sheer battle to overcome my natural sedentary tendencies followed by throbbing bones, torn ligaments and aching muscles did prove to be the distraction I'd hoped for; as did the smell of A535.

Then I had children and suddenly no longer had to worry about hitching too long a ride on any train of thought. Best I can do these days is one zone, after that the train gets rerouted to a siding by "Dad, how long are you going to be? I need to poo," or "Dad, are you being a writer right now, or just watching TV?" or "Look Dad. Look. Look-it. Look-it!"

Having thought all of these thoughts, I wanted to take down some notes but I was in the bath and didn't have my smartphone, but knew that I probably wouldn't have used it anyway as I prefer paper and pen. From here I started thinking about how I don't text while I drive because that would be dangerous, but instead when brilliance strikes, I scramble for a pen while steering with one hand, one eye on the road. Then I thought about how the clipboard suction-cupped to my dash recently broke which means that I have to scramble for paper, too, and so, in the throes of brilliance, I will now have to drive with the steering wheel between my teeth. It's almost inevitable that someday, my kids will be able to exclaim, "There's Daddy's car, again, on YouTube!"

Broken things reminded me that we are only three weeks away from leaving for Japan to see my wife's family and I have so much left to do before I go. I'm taking my parents with us on this trip and I thought of the hilarity that will ensue when my father is faced with such things as raw egg on noodles—or, in fact, even just noodles. He's always said he'd never travel to any country that didn't have a Domino's Pizza! Of all the pizza in the world, why Domino's? No idea. Why a benevolent, bearded white man looking down from the clouds? Apparently, it really doesn't take much to start the ideology ball rolling.

To be fair, Dad credits Domino's Pizza with saving his life in Mexico—while staying in an all-inclusive resort with my sister,

Dad: [grumbling] Nothing tastes the same here.
Sister: Are you saying that all of this Mexican food tastes foreign? Strange that.
Dad: Something's off.
Sister : [exasperated sigh] Dad, it's a Mars bar.
Dad: Now, *there's* a sign.
Sister: Of senility, perhaps?
Dad: Over there. That sign—Domino's Pizza. Finally, something Canadian!
Sister: Their head office is in Michigan. When did Michigan become part of Canada?
Dad: About the same time that Nacho chips became supper.

You wouldn't think so, but Dad's a survivor. He'll probably stuff his pockets with M&M's at the airport and actually gain weight in Japan. And, perhaps, start a new religion.

Anyway, I looked it up and Japan does have Domino's Pizza. It's a bit of a shame, really, as I could possibly get on board an M&M-based religion but it would depend on what's at the heart of the religion: peanut or chocolate. I could not worship a peanut God. That would be ridiculous.

This all led to how much my father will enjoy it when my Japanese father-in-law takes him gambling. Though they have no common language they actually get on very well which sometimes makes me wish that my wife and I didn't share a common language. (She often claims we don't. At least, I think that's what she's saying.) Neither man can understand the other but they especially seem to enjoy gambling together although it almost certainly means that one of them has no clue how to play the games. I guess it's fortunate that losing can be competently achieved without knowledge.

That made me realize that there is no way that I will be able to interpret gambling lingo between my father and father-in-law.

Then I remembered my own two gambling experiences in Japan and I chuckled.

So now I'm writing about gambling in Japan. But I've gone on so long following this loosely associated jumble of thoughts that I'll have to save that for a later article.

Such is the muddled mind of a writer.

Sorry you had to see that.

Though a convenience for most, the smartphone can be a big inconvenience for writers of fiction.

Writing a good novel and getting it to press is a long process. It took less than five years for the smartphone to go from fantasy to everyday reality, altering almost every aspect of daily life. Novels written five years ago need to be updated. What might once have been a present-day action adventure story must now be declared to have taken place in the past, if the characters aren't glued to their smartphones. Something written ten years ago is now a "period piece."

The first novel I ever wrote is still unpublished, largely because of this. It's a science-fiction action story about a high-tech detective who is physically wired to the Internet. I finished writing it in 2004 and started shopping it around to publishers. No takers. About five years ago, it became obvious that technology had evolved and my story needed updating. On my first re-read, I became depressed, realizing that I might as well replace every occurrence of my protagonist's name with the word, "smartphone." Also, I'd need to rename it: "A Smartphone Called Intrepid."

Beyond their frantic evolutionary cycles, Smartphones challenge authors in that they are too convenient and remove too many obstacles. Scenes like exhaustive research in a library, or flipping through a phone book for leads have been contracted into a couple of swipes on a screen. Having immediate and private access to everything also isolates your characters, reducing the opportunity for chance encounters and unexpected twists. As simple a plot device as being lost has become a complicated event to arrange, with any realism.

In order for a protagonist to get in to a real jam, an author has to deprive him of the ability to call for help. But now that phones are actually pocket computers, he also has to lose the ability to look things up on the internet, use GPS and maps, camera, email and social media, which means that somewhere in the course of the story, the author must set aside time to have the smartphone lost, destroyed, damaged or electronically blocked. As a last ditch effort, a writer can arrange to have the battery run out, but that often makes the hero look like an idiot for not having charged it; similar to tripping over a tree root or running upstairs to escape a crazed killer.

Outside of books, I really notice the effect in recent Bond movies. James spends far less time with Q than he used to, because otherwise we'd end up with scenes like this...

> **Q:** You'll want to keep this close, 007. It's a communication device, but also a set of encyclopaedia, universal translator, GPS, minicomputer and plumb bob.
> **Bond:** It appears to be an iPhone.
> **Q:** Quite right. Mind you don't get it wet.
> **Bond:** Couldn't I just use mine?
> **Q:** Ours is on AT&T.
> **Bond:** Verizon: 100 Megabit, unlimited roaming.
> **Q:** I see. Best use yours, then.

And, of course, the obligatory capture scene would also need to be brought up to speed...

Dr. Evil Genius [bent of world domination]: Mr. Bond, the reason I have just spent the better part of a half hour revealing to you all the intricate details of my plan is that you won't be around to stop me, as you'll soon be quite dead. This death ray is pointed directly at your genitals, strapped as you are to this operating table I conveniently keep in the middle of my living room. When the candle breaks that string, a ping pong ball will fall out of that cup and roll along this ruler until it reaches that set of dominoes. As the dominoes fall they will strike a match which will, in turn, light a fuse detonating a fire cracker launching a lead fishing weight into that rolling pin, causing it to hit this shiny red button thus activating the completely redundant timer which will fire the death ray in precisely 13 seconds. Pity I can't stay to enjoy the show. Oh, and by the way, no sense trying to escape: I've jammed your cell provider. Also, my wifi network is password protected.

Bond: You've wasted a lot of effort, then, Doctor Genius. My battery's dead.

If smartphones are ever updated to include explosives and oil slicks, it's all over for Q and evil geniuses.

And, if I ever see James Bond take a selfie, it's all over for me, as well.

William M. Dean: Writer
- Yes, I am poor.
- No, I do not wish that I had written "_____."
- Yes, I am aware that no one reads anymore.
- No, I am not drunk.

14 Unexpected
After-You-Publish Moments

If you are an indie author, like me, several things may happen after you publish—most of them unexpected.

1) Your friends might say, "I bought your book. I'm already on chapter eighteen and can't wait to finish it." But, they are more apt to say, "I started your book and I'm almost all the way through chapter one," as if, due to the tediousness of the task, this is an outstanding achievement. Then, afraid that you might continually check on their progress, they will add, "I plan to read a paragraph a day." Making you wonder how your playful action/adventure story could burn people out like this.

In March, my sister and her family decided to read a chapter of my novel at the dinner table every time they all got together. Her kids are young adults with school, jobs and active social lives. Turns out, they are hardly ever all assembled at dinner, at the same time. Two months later, they reached chapter four. *Because they are my family with a genetic disposition to being silly, and perhaps because they were all home schooled, they had decided to act each scene out, as they read. When they came to the part where the protagonist has sex with a nun, there was an awkward silence and progress such as it was, ground to a halt.*

2) The statement from your friend: "I'm giving every one of my friends a copy of your book as a Christmas present, this year," will eventually make you wonder if you are their only friend.

3) You watch your book sit at 100,000th ranking on Amazon for a week as all of your friends and relatives purchase. Then it begins to sink. It hits 1,000,000th and you feel you've probably hit rock bottom. Then, suddenly, you're at 5,000,000th.

How low can it go? Well, the lowest ranked Amazon's book I could find was at 12 million.

In general, you'll probably bottom out at about 5-6 millionth mark. Amazon uses a complex algorithm to determine rank, but to sink much lower your book will have to have absolutely no sales and no relevance to any living person.

Apparently, Amazon has over 17 million books in its database, although the highest (lowest?) number ranking claimed to have been seen is around fourteen millionth. If my math is correct—never a given—then this means that a book ranked 500,000th is in the upper three percent. At five millionth, your book is still in the top thirty percent of all the books in Amazon's database!

4) You will check your stats and discover that you have sold about five percent of the books that you thought, based on the people who told you they'd bought a copy and hits on your website. It will make you suspect the entire Amazon system. It could be the system. But probably not. In either case, you have no ability to truly audit that system. Move on.

5) You will continue to update your blog and think about the next big novel. Though your writing is clever and you make yourself laugh a lot, you will continue to have only four blog followers. Friends will read the first paragraph of the first blog with a title that catches their interest. One day, you will come across a Facebook friend who you vaguely know who has actually read all of your blogs. This will be at once flattering and depressing as there are good reasons that the two of you are not close.

Meanwhile, a friend's eight-year-old daughter will start a blog about how she likes to play with My Little Pony figures and, almost overnight, will get 150,000 hits. YouTube will email, begging her to monetize her videos.

6) You will come to realize just how much time writing robs you from your family and other less stressful pursuits and wonder how foolish you are to keep pursuing it for no money.

A good friend and fellow writer recently said, "If doing the same thing over and over and expecting different results is the definition of insanity, then by definition, publishing a second novel is insane."

7) People will start introducing you as an author which will make you blush and confused because it sounds so pretentious and yet it's true and so few people actually write a novel—and yet it has cost you more money than it's made and more time than it will likely ever be worth. And yet, it's still true. And yet, you're still a greeter at Wal-Mart.

8) After being introduced as an author, it will become apparent how few people read these days. You will realize that your book is trying to reach a niche market that is part of a market that is already niche: "Those who still read books."

9) You will be elected to write a commencement speech for your niece's graduation ceremony and suddenly, because you are now a "writer" the pressure will be immense and you'll get writer's block and stall and pray she fails her finals but will end up writing a decent speech, three days before the event. Performing to expectations that no one but you actually have will also require half a bottle of Sake.

10) People will offer you story ideas as if a lack of ideas is the thing stopping you from rattling off a hundred blockbuster novels. In fact, too many ideas pulling you in fifty directions at once is more the problem. Fortunately, their ideas will not add to your problem because they all suck. Only you have the truly good ideas.

11) One day, you may be scrolling through Facebook posts—which, by the way, may well be a valid part of the writing process, for all anyone knows—and find that you have a fan. Try to remain calm. Remember that some people sniff lighter fluid for entertainment.

12) You will frequent coffee shops and talk loudly about writing and literature so that pretty young girls sitting close by might overhear and think of you as intriguing and, perhaps, sexy as opposed to somebody's perverted granddad. The pretty young girls can't hear you

William M Dean shared Roundhouse Café's photo.
July 29 at 9:05pm · 🌐 ▼

(wmdean.com) I have a fan! A verified fan! (Honest, this post was not photoshopped.)

Roundhouse Café

Having a Beetroot Mango Smoothie, enjoying the sunshine and a good book (The Space Between Thought) by William M. Dean at the Roundhouse Cafe...Can't get any better than that!

14 Likes

👍 Like   💬 Comment   ↪ Share

because they have earbuds in under their long, silky, blond hair. You will notice this as they get up to move to a table out of your line of sight.

13) After 8 months of diligently blogging you wonder if you are missing a huge opportunity by not monetize your blog, using Google Adsense. So you will let Google place ads alongside in return for which Google will automatically set aside cash for you, based on the number of clicks they generate. Two months later, you will check on your earnings. They will be twenty-four cents.

14) One day, while you sit writing in your office, you go online to research something and discover that someone who read your book has pulled a quote and pasted the words over a suitable background picture and released it online. You are suddenly proud to have slaved over your novel and happy to now be sitting in your office slaving over the next one. Also, you have a steaming cup of coffee with a generous dose of Bailey's Irish Cream close by. And you're naked.

Hey, if you have to be working on a Sunday...

23

One Author's Man Cave

The fumes still make me high, and I feel sorry for all the silverfish I displaced. I later popped a window in behind the monitors which surely surprised my neighbor whose house is about 20 feet away.

It's taken me nine years to scavenge a small chuck of real estate within my house; a private area to sit and read or write, and which does not contain a toilet.

I do miss the gentle whisper of the fan.

Until now, whenever I wrote, my children were playing at my feet. Eventually, I would tire of reading the same sentence over and over and would retreat to the bathroom where I might possibly absorb or generate a new thought, between repeated knocks on the door. One day, reading on the toilet while *"I Miss You, Daddy"* notes slid under the door and gathered at my feet, I realized that I had become a cliché. I like to fit in, but not in this way.

Why did it take me nine years to construct an eight-foot-square sanctuary? Mostly, I was busy renovating and doubling the size of our house; a six-month project that took eight years—unless you count trivial finishing touches like doorknobs and light switches, in which case it's still ongoing and likely to be complete about two days before we retire and decide to downsize. My wife, Junko, was not impressed with the timeline. I blame Mike Holmes for her unrealistic expectations.

About two years ago, we were invited to a friend's house. Junko and I tried to figure out just what made theirs seem like such a better house than ours. Eventually it struck us: This house has moldings!

We'd lived so long without moldings that we'd completely forgotten about them—until that day. After that, it became a priority for Junko. I argued with her about this, but I'm not sure why—not sure why I argue, in general. The outcome never varies. Moldings became a priority for me.

I think that Junko expected the moldings project to start with me obtaining some molding and nailing it along the edges of the walls. Why is it so difficult for wives to grasp the simple fact that in order to do moldings, you obviously have to start by renovating the attic?

Trust me. I've got eight years of experience.

When you renovate a space occupied by a family of four, you spend most of your time clearing space, finding your tools, gathering them at the project site and then cleaning up afterward. The actual work takes place in that tiny space between the above words "then" and "cleaning" but is not a large enough part of the process to warrant inclusion in the sentence.

Tackling an entire house-worth of moldings meant finishing the fireplace because the moldings butt up against it. To finish the fireplace I needed all my tools which, at that point, were dispersed throughout the house, close to wherever they were last used. In order to find them, and to give me access to the walls that I was going to work on, I needed to move all the storage boxes that we had cleverly incorporated into our home decor. Our coffee table was an orange crate full of books with a doily-like afghan over it. In order to move the storage boxes, I needed a place to put them. This meant laying down a floor in the attic.

Obviously, after the attic, comes the garage renovation, so that I have somewhere to organize and store my tools. Then I could finish the fireplace, and only then, would it become possible to do the moldings.

It took several months. But my renovating speed and efficiency surged forward after all of my tools were organized, in the garage. I even managed to fit in side projects like building a Free Little Library, bathroom cabinet, several large bookshelves, separate bedrooms for the kids, and two tree houses.

The moldings, themselves, took about a day. Junko was expressionless and quiet. As she is Japanese, this could either mean she was appropriately impressed or incredibly upset that she had waited nine years for a one-day project. When I talk about renovations now, her left eye no longer twitches. Well, not as much. So I'm assuming she was impressed.

Junko was also impressed with the gusto with which I tackled all of this. What she didn't realize—what I was clever enough not to mention—was that none of this was about moldings. All of this was really about my man cave. Until the attic was organized, there was no place to build myself the sanctuary I needed to sustain my writing.

As soon as the last molding was nailed in place, I climbed the ladder back into the attic and began to ponder a little eight-by-eight wooden box suited to accommodating pure genius.

For scale, Noah is about four feet tall. The door is a bit "Hobbit-y" and I bump my head twice a day, which may go some distance in explaining some of the stuff I produce.

Our living space had become storage-box-free over the last few months. Consequently, we now had about a thousand boxes in the attic. There was absolutely no room to work. Some boxes had to be brought downstairs long enough for me to complete this project.

Trust in a marriage is a good thing. I brought about twenty boxes filled with Christmas decorations downstairs and explained to Junko that sometimes, in Canada, Christmas festivities begin in October. It's for occasions such as these that I work hard to build trust, the rest of the time. Having a Japanese wife unsure of North American traditions may have helped sell the concept, but an interesting thing about my wife is that she might not believe anything I say, but if challenging it will not affect the outcome, she pretends to accept it at face value—a reaction that I choose to accept at face value. At any rate, she never protested the early intrusion into our living space, the man cave construction project was able to proceed and the Christmas season started three months early, that year.

With more than 100,000 views on my blog and 6000 Twitter "followers," I am many times more famous than I ever dreamed I'd be—though far less rich. Of course, for the most part, my Twitter fans are Israeli spammers, but I'm also a pretty big online deal with Turkish bots.

I'm virtually a superstar, but it's entirely possible that I am my only actual fan.

Still, I enjoy the illusion that I created something of value and that the proof lies somewhere in those numbers—or at least, some fraction of those numbers. Possibly, a single digit. (*Thanks, Mom!*) But it feels like something akin to validation though this may just be my personal version of clapping for Tinker Bell.

About forty years ago, I read a science fiction novel predicting a future in which every individual was incorporated. I remember thinking that the idea was as ridiculous as bottled water. Turns out, I was right. But things did not play out as expected. Bottled water is now commonplace and almost every individual is very clearly selling something: their imaginary lifestyle, their "perfect" relationship, their exciting job, their trendy lunch or some product or service. Need proof? Next time you're stuck in traffic, check the neighboring cars. A large percentage will bear magnetic advertisements on their doors, stickers in their windows, or at the least a bumper sticker: Proud Parent, I Love NY, Trump for Ex-President 2017, stick-figure family—including pets and ex-wife.

I get it. I'm a writer. I'd love to sell a book or two. And I know that I should be relentlessly shouting the news to anyone who will listen. But I just can't make myself spam the world or beg my friends to read my stuff. In fact, it's best they never find out that I write about them.

I am also aware of the flip side of writing—a sort of pyramid scheme in which you achieve the dream by selling the dream. But, I have no urge to use my books as a pedestal from which to preach writer-gospel to fellow struggling writers. If I were to offer a course to writers, it would not be inspirational. I'd start by telling them that writing is all about personal gratification through a largely imaginary lifestyle, and definitely not about money. I'd add that it's going to cost them time, energy, probably a relationship or two and some of that money that it's not about. No book is ever going to spontaneously generate an income, or if it does, when you look back you will decide that it was not worth the time and effort. Your ascent will be a long-tailed curve of sacrifices through which you emerge less a victor than a survivor. If, after hearing all this, they still want to be writers, then I would congratulate them, because they already are. True writers have no choice but to write. After that, it might be fun to award coffee mugs, which are equally suitable for alcoholic beverages and receiving charitable donations—or maybe ascots.

The writer's lifestyle that many of us imagine is a stress-free, peaceful existence with loads of idle time spent basking in the validation of fans and the admiration of peers—oh, and debt-free. Well, I have kids. So for me, "stress-free" and "peaceful" are non-starters. Both the word "basking" and the word "fans" seem hyperbolic. And so few would admit to being my peer that admiration is unlikely. I am debt-free—but only briefly, twice a month, when I get my day-job pay check. Well, one out of five ain't bad. Great news: I've achieved 20 percent, and it only took two-thirds of my life! The future looks... inadequate.

While writing is art, writing for money is business and the sad fact is that, for most of us, the stuff that sells is not very satisfying to write—it is not literary music and does not expose deep truths. The vast majority of money-making, popular materials are either products of the social media echo chamber which knows what you like and what you like to believe and rehashes it through popular memes, or ones that seek to play seeing-eye-dog to our blind ambitions, usually premised on exaggerated claims bent on luring us out into rush hour traffic.

If, by chance, you're already a popular writer, then you've gotten a grasp of the game and become good at it. Generally, that involves volume, because an endless supply of product is what keeps the money flowing. Money, itself, is of much less value than people think; it's the rate of flow that measures success. The reality of being a popular writer is not the lifestyle you are probably imagining. It's a lot less time spent stringing beautiful words than coaxing a mundane concept into too little space, or sacrificing eloquence in order to save content, or chugging out credible-sounding drivel because that's what really pays.

The most successful writer I know, personally, creates top-ten-style websites based on Google search requests. He picks a popular search topic, writes what is basically advertising material that sounds like first-hand advice and adds pictures with links to the products. He collects a few cents every time his material inspires someone to click one of the links. If they actually purchase a product he gets the equivalent of me selling ten paperback books. In a single month, his writing generates more than mine does in a year.

They say that if you want to be successful you have to want it "bad enough." I have found this to be very true. I never wanted anything bad enough to do what many of the more successful people around me were willing to. I've never wanted to risk anyone else's money, talk up a product beyond realistic expectations, make promises I couldn't keep, or sacrifice my health. Of course, I did all of those things, but only for the first few years after entering the job market. Those I know who did not alter course have been financially rewarded. I'm not the least bitter. I would have done the same if I could have ignored my core beliefs. I blame Walt Disney who, ironically, built his empire feeding people like me a hobbling set of core beliefs.

As we age, it's more difficult to achieve success because the accumulation of knowledge and experience tends to yield self-awareness and empathy, which is akin to tossing a juggler an anvil. No longer blinded by ambition, we become less able to exaggerate, manipulate, gouge or steal and still hold our heads up. We may still feel the urge to climb that social ladder, but now we are hobbled, while those younger and brasher crush our fingers in their rush to the next rung. If they're lucky, they'll only regret this much later, while poolside, sipping margaritas.

In my own days of youthful ignorance, I made quite a bit of money. At twenty-seven, I was bringing in $60,000 a year as a publisher. My wife, at the time, was doing equally well and together we quickly built a small empire. When I look back at what I had to do in order to manage my staff I now see much of it as manipulating, lying and cheating. I could never do this today. In fact, I wasn't really very good at it, even back then. At thirty-five I chose to step out of the management stream in which I had been paddling. For about fourteen years I sold sandwiches, which I saw as the least harmful thing I could possibly do. The product was food and the choice was simple: You either wanted a ham and cheese or you didn't. I didn't have to convince anyone to buy. And I didn't have to sacrifice my health because it was physical enough that it provided a decent workout, four hours a day. Oh yeah, and it was only four hours a day! I truly enjoyed that job. Since then, I have accumulated many more assets, but that was the time in my life that I felt the most satisfied with my lot.

All I ever wanted to do was create something cool without doing any harm and maintain a living while doing it. A pretty modest goal, twenty percent of which I have achieved. The only element completely missing is validation. And, even more than money, I think that is what most of us are desperately looking for.

I clearly understand the need, but I get tired of being sold to. Everyone wants my validation, or my money so that they can purchase the validation of others—or they want both. It used to be that to escape the sales pitches all you had to do was leave the mall and shut off your TV. These days, you have to stop communicating with your friends, as well.

I guess I'm no different. My writing is my product, but it is also my advertisement.

But, I have to write. In fact, I can only suppress the urge for a short while before my mind seems to become fragmented, I feel anxious and ungrounded. At that point, I must find a keyboard, a pen and pad, or write in blood on the back of an envelope. This is how I stumble my way back to a calm. I am not the least encumbered by the fact that I might have nothing to say. I guess we call this "writing" and not "informing" for the same reason that we go "fishing" and not "catching."

A few weeks ago, my wife felt that we were drifting apart. She wanted us to start having a half-hour tea-time together, each night. I jumped at the offer because, first of all, it is atypically romantic of her, and secondly,

I thought there might be biscuits. Well, three weeks later, the romance has worn thin, the half-hour lasts about an hour and a half and our discussions are teaching us that we don't agree on as much as we thought. Also, there are no biscuits and I now have to get up at three in the morning to pee. Tea-time has all but eliminated my writing time and my wife is so much more devious than romantic that I have to wonder if this was not the actual intent. She's always seemed very supportive of my writing, but that's exactly what a devious person would want me to think. Argh! I am fragmented, anxious and ungrounded.

And this is entirely why I had to write tonight, without any topic in mind.

Even though I do wear a cardigan, maybe I'm not actually a writer. Maybe I'm just a rant-addict selling myself as a writer. Sometimes, a sweater is just a sweater.

Regardless, here I remain, anxiously awaiting your validation.

Addendum:

It's 3am and I had to get up to pee. It's not such an inconvenience. Tonight is one of those nights when my mind is churning and sleep is fitful. I'm feeling creative. I grab a pad of paper and proceed to the toilet. I'm scribbling away with my favourite pen when the cap pops off and falls between my legs. Plop! Before the last ripple settles I deftly pluck the top from the urine and toss it across the room and into the sink, impressed by the cat-likeness of my reflexes and the deadliness of my accuracy. Then I remember: Earlier today, I was teaching my daughter about how her hair clogs our sink and I removed the stopper. It's 3:30am and I am disassembling my bathroom sink to retrieve the cap to my favourite pen. This is a writer's lifestyle.

25

Don't Panic!

It's Just JAPAN

It's a popular Internet meme that strange and Japan are synonymous. But then, Donald Trump became President of the United States. So, who are we to judge?

Junko and I travel to Japan about every four years, and for me, all the important things are similar and only the inconsequential things are different. But, those inconsequential things can be surprising. Even though I now have a deeper understanding, a trip to Japan is still as exotic and exciting as it was the first time, and the wonder and strangeness never seem to fade.

Below, is a list of the differences that I most noticed when I first set foot in Japan. As with every other such list of peculiarities, this one will prepare you for Japan much in the same way that basting prepares the turkey to enjoy a happy Thanksgiving.

In and Around the Home:

- I was not surprised by the automated toilet seats, as their existence is now widely known. However, I was surprised how quickly I got used to it and how badly I wanted one for my own house. Ten years later, I have one and can say with confidence that only a toddler's butt could be more pampered, and that, in every sense of the phrase, I have probably written much more than is justified on the Japanese toilet.

- Japanese toilets have a small faucet and basin above the cistern. After you flush, the incoming water is used for washing your hands.

- In most houses, toilet and washing up areas are separated. This means some rearranging of daily hygiene rituals.

- The shower and bathtub are together in a waterproof room. You are expected to wash using the shower and relax in the tub. Family and guests all share the same bathwater, which is recycled, cleaned and

replenished via a computerized system. The bathtub is drained periodically for cleaning, but otherwise stays full and warm, with an insulated cover over top to save energy.

- Many of the homes I've visited have both Western- and Japanese-style, living rooms. In the traditional Japanese-style living room, the table stands in a square pit that has an electric heater at the bottom. The duvet-like blanket is called a *kotatsu* and is used to conserve the heat, during colder weather. In most Japanese homes, this is as close to central heating and insulation as you are going to get.

- Slippers are a big deal. The entranceway to every home has a tiled area below floor level dedicated to the idea. You are expected to doff your shoes there and then slip into guest slippers to cross the wooden floors of the rest of the home. At the entrance to the bathroom will be yet another pair of special, rubber slippers. You back out of your guest slippers and slip into these while using the toilet. I found it arduous to change upon entering every room and

Common Japanese residential architecture. The building is raised off the ground, the exterior walls are thinner than in North America, and most interior walls are either paper or some sort of thin hardboard material. The roof is heavy ceramic tile.

eventually gave up. Being Caucasian gives you some license to ignore tradition and get away with it.

- Most Japanese homes have no insulation or central heat. The idea is to heat bodies, not rooms. In cold weather, they wear layers and eat hot foods. A lot of leisure time is spent around the Japanese living room table; your lower body huddled under the *kotatsu*, while an electric heating unit warms your toes, from below.

- You will find only cooking knives in Japanese kitchens. There are few, if any, butter knives, and nothing like a steak knife. The cook is expected to serve the meal with everything pre-sliced and diced, convenient for eating with chopsticks.

- Japanese housewives grocery shop, daily. I'm uncertain whether this is cause or effect, but Japanese households are not built for stockpiling. Fridges and cupboards are one-third the size of the American equivalent.

- In Japan, the traditional family culture is very strong and includes a stay-at-home mom. In this arrangement, the women control the purse strings and do the majority of the purchasing, so businesses have found it in their best interest to make shopping as convenient as possible for housewives with toddlers. The most obvious example is the prevalence of large, kid-oriented amusement centers in department stores. Often, they employ an attendant—or, more recently, a robot—to supervise the children. The price is always so reasonable that it becomes unreasonable *not* to utilize the service. This is quite opposite of the Western idea of charging parents through the nose for things their kids desire.

- **TV:** The language barrier never seems so high as when you watch Japanese television. Almost every program introduces some element that seems bizarre and requires an explanation. After a while, you just go for a walk.

    Beyond a clutter of garish typewritten comments pasted over just about every show, a small box is often inset in one corner featuring the face of a celebrity guest watching the same thing that you are watching. His/her reaction to the material is meant to help you appreciate, in the proper way, the content; like the laugh track in an American comedy. The celebrities can be seen reacting to what is on the screen which helps set the context for the audience; they laugh when it's supposed to be funny and make appropriate exclamations when something is surprising, horrific, or looks tasty.

When watching news and current-affairs programs you will notice that broadcasters still use paper charts with peel and stick labels as much as they use computer graphics. This reflects a long tradition of cleverly utilizing paper.

Collage of images from a variety of typical Japanese TV programs. In the lower image, one man whips another, between the legs. Go figure.

- Outdoor banks of vending machines are a common sight in every neighborhood. They may be found wherever there is power and some shelter, and are almost as common on rural back roads as they are on urban thoroughfares. Most dispense juice, coffee, tea and cigarettes, but I've also seen ones that sell comic books, condoms, and even one offering a variety of household objects like brushes, screwdrivers, rubber bands and light bulbs. An urban legend persists that Japanese vending machines sell used panties. This has some basis in fact: For a brief time there were a few such machines, but then new laws were made to address the disturbing practice, and those few machines disappeared.

Food:
- If you look up the world's fifty weirdest foods, via Google, you will find that Japan corner's the market with eight contributions,

including a couple of dishes served alive and moving. The Japanese are obsessed with food and have a very broad palate. They are also obsessively polite. Consequently, *"Oishi!"* (delicious!) is the most commonly used Japanese word.

• If you ever host a Japanese visitor, you need to know that they are not used to using knives to eat their meals. I realized this the first time my Japanese father-in-law visited Canada and I took him out for dinner with a group of friends. He does not speak English and could not read the menu, so I ordered a steak for him. I was almost finished my meal before noticing that he hadn't taken a bite of his steak. And that's when it dawned on me that, in Japan, everything is served already cut, suitable for chopsticks. He had no experience wielding a knife in such a precise manner and I guess he felt too self-conscious to take a "stab" at it. I surreptitiously sliced it up for him. We were both slightly embarrassed.

• Generally, it is not impolite to slurp your soup. I'm so westernized that I was unable to do this without spraying the room with noodle drippings. The family was surprised that I lacked this basic culinary skill.

• Restaurants—including many fast food places—will give you a wet napkin to wash your hands with, before a meal. It's gauche to wash your face with this.

- Generally, restaurants do not supply paper napkins. They assume you carry tissue with you and can use that. When licking my fingers doesn't cut it, I steal the toilet paper and try to keep it hidden.

- A related observation: There are no paper towels in most restaurant bathrooms.

- Japanese ice cream, pizza toppings candy and potato chip flavors include things like wasabi, seaweed, squid, shrimp and corn.

- I never saw anyone eating anything while walking—not even a candy bar or a hot dog. I have since learned that it is considered rude. The Japanese always take their food somewhere, and sit to enjoy it.

- I noticed that corn seems inordinately relished, though it is a common vegetable, in Japan.

- Many things in Japan are about one-third smaller than in North America, but not beer. It's served in mugs that are about one and a half times larger than what we get here.

A familiar thing with unfamiliar falvors: Apple Pie Kit Kat and Matcha Tea Kit Kat. It's worth noting that potato chips are more likely to be nori- (sea weed) or sushi-flavored than, say, salted.

- **Finance:** Cash is still the most common transaction. Credit cards are still not accepted in a lot of places, even where they expect tourists. And banks still verify your identity by a personal family ink stamp, called an *inkan*, a practice I had never heard of, before I went to Japan.

- **Real Estate:** In the rural area where I've spent most of my time, houses either look completely dilapidated or brand new. Old houses are abandoned or bulldozed rather than renovated. My father-in-law's fifty-year-old house had been constructed from forty-foot spans of clear timber that, these days, only the wealthiest people could afford. A few years ago, that lumber was hauled away and burned before they started construction of his new house. The idea of renovating an existing structure seems to only now be gaining traction, probably due to the extended economic downturn.

- **Tourism:** In cosmopolitan areas like Tokyo, the Japanese are making strides in accommodating English-speaking tourists. However, their efforts are still unevenly applied; mostly amounting to English

Door to door milk delivery is still available. In the summer, the milk is left in a cooler, with ice packs.

signage. You may well follow English signs to a bilingual ticket agent and book a three-hour guided tour only to find that your guide speaks only Japanese. I would not yet say that Japan is a comfortable destination for English-speakers.

- **Relaxation:** The *Onsen* is a traditional Japanese public bath, designed for relaxation. They are ubiquitous throughout Japan and a very common form of recreation. *Onsen* feature large, communal hot tubs in which people bathe, naked. Men and women usually bathe in separate facilities. If you go, expect to be gawked at by Japanese children.

On my last trip, I noticed two strange things that I had never noticed before. The first thing was that, in the change room, the other men tended to cover their private parts with a small towel, even though we were all male, and all soon to be exposed.

Onsen, like all Japanese baths, are exclusively for relaxation, not for cleaning. So, before entering any Japanese bath you are expected to wash and rinse your body. At an *Onsen,* this is part of the relaxation process and performed both thoroughly and leisurely.

The second thing I noticed was that after sweating in hot water, no one washes, on the way out. I thought this odd, considering the Japanese obsession with cleanliness.

A hand-cranked paper shredder. I've never seen one, outside of Japan.

Driving:
- As in North America, a green light in Japan is green. However, they call it "blue."

- Cars and streets are about one-third smaller than in North America. Therefore, city maps look more crowded.

- The streets are so narrow and tight that there are a lot of blind corners, so you'll notice a lot of mirrors mounted at corners... it's the only way to know if someone is about to enter the intersection.

- Drivers almost always back into parking spots.

- There are no street signs or house numbers in my in-laws' large, rural neighborhood. I still have no idea how the mail gets delivered—or a pizza, for that matter.

- In an emergency, you dial 1-1-9 instead of 9-1-1.

Language:
- Perhaps the most obvious thing is that the language is a barrier. But what surprised me, and may surprise you, is just how high that barrier is. Not only will you not be able to understand or participate in conversations, but you will be unable to read. Sometimes, just choosing the right bathroom will be a challenge. This reduces you to the dependency level of a four-year-old

- A Japanese-English dictionary has no "L" section.

The People:
- In Canada, my five-foot, nine inches (175 cm) is about average and a lot of men are taller than me, so, the first time I visited Japan, I looked forward to being the tallest one in a crowd and imagined myself being able to see over the all the heads. But, in the very first entirely Japanese crowd I encountered in Tokyo, all of the younger men were at least as tall as me, and most were taller. I did tower over the average woman, though. Turns out, that due to dietary

improvements, the younger generations tend to be taller. The average height in Japan is currently five foot eight inches (173 cm) and increasing, each year.

- As well as increasing their height, a more modern diet, which now includes frozen and fast foods, has resulted in a visible number of overweight people. I have noticed the difference over the fifteen years I've been traveling to Japan. Based on observations made during my last trip, I'd say that about 20% of the under-30 population is now above an ideal weight.

- Japanese women admire pale-skinned, Western beauty. They try to stay out of the sun to keep their skin youthful, and rely on long gloves, umbrellas or even skin whiteners to emulate the Western look. Their efforts to adhere to this ideal prevent them from being outdoorsy.

- Public displays of affection are frowned upon. Younger people are demonstrative enough to hold hands, but older people—including my own wife, while we're in Japan—would be embarrassed by this. I never saw any other form of touching in public.

- Japanese will praise you highly for the least achievement. Do not let it go to your head. They don't mean it. They are measuring the humility in your response. They like humility.

- The Japanese are masters of understatement and self-deprecation. If a Japanese person says that they have taken a Karate lesson then you may expect that they are, in fact, a first-degree black belt. Foreigners who exaggerate their abilities constantly amuse them. So, unless you are fluent, I would not mention that you know some Japanese. If you always understate your abilities, you will be better received.

- If you are a foreigner, you are exempt from almost every rule: That you behave strangely is a given. However the Japanese appreciate any attempt to learn their language and accommodate to their customs.

- When a toddler loses a tooth they throw it on top or under the house: Lower tooth on the roof so it grows a healthy replacement, straight down, and upper teeth under the house so it grows a healthy replacement, upward. Go figure. Not sure what they do when Grandpa loses his teeth.

- The Japanese are profoundly practical. When faced with a religious decision between Shinto and Buddhism, they generally choose both. Japanese homes often have two separate shrines. Perhaps frustrating to religions everywhere, the Japanese see no hypocrisy in selecting bits and pieces that they like from each religion. This may be the single wisest thing I have ever heard.

Strange-English clothing items for children: Teen clothing, especially, often attempts to be edgy but instead ends up inappropriately adult. One toddler's shirt I saw, read: "Call me, bitch!"

148

My kids are remarkably quiet, respectful, well behaved and smart. I started having kids late in life and I like to think that my maturity and wisdom had some impact, but they probably get all the good stuff from their mother's side of the family.

Regardless, I have gathered all that I have learned as a parent and compressed it into this top-10 list. Yes, I know there are actually 45 things in the list, nevertheless, this is a top-10 list... with bonus material, because the modern world is not interested in top-45 lists. Also, there are 46.

1) Advice Regarding Advice: Among the first things that come with the parenting experience is a strong set of opinions about parenting accompanied by a looming sense of guilt that you may be failing your child in some way. Children are cute and attract a lot of attention wherever they go, so to add to this self-inflicted pressure is the fact that all the eyes of society are upon you and judging you by your child's behavior. So my very first advice to a parent is to resist shaming or criticizing another parent. Their strong opinions will collide with yours and that sense of possible guilt will make them defensive and likely volatile. Unless they ask, never tell another parent how to raise their kids. And if they ask, be gentle. It's the hardest criticism to take and you may not know what you are talking about. Feel the overwhelming urge to share? Do what I do: write a blog that few read.

2) One thing to keep in mind that will help you sympathize with the parents of "wayward" children is that **kids are born with natural dispositions firmly in place.** Some of those built-in tendencies do not fit well into society and it can be a long and delicate task to redirect this innate behavior without breaking the child's spirit.

3) **Your children will act out, behave in bizarre ways or blurt inappropriate things in public.** Try not to worry what others think because your kids can detect this and use your discomfort as a tool to get what they want. Remember: People who haven't raised children have no clue. People who have are probably sympathetic. Those unwise enough to judge you are not wise enough to competently advise you.

4) **Yelling is ineffective.** The one thing that kids crave above all

else is your attention. And they don't discriminate between good and bad attention, the way an adult might. So when you yell at your kids for misbehaving, you may actually be rewarding their little reptile brains and encouraging their antics. For this reason, they are unlikely to stop jumping on the couch just because you yelled at them.

5) Actions speak louder than words. If their misbehavior is physically interrupted, kids consider that a negative thing. Instead of yelling, get off your butt and stop them.

6) Follow through on your threats. This way, you'll be more careful about using threats and your children will learn to respect your authority. People who yell at their kids, but never physically enforce their threats, have children who ignore them. And, they end up yelling a lot. You can't parent from a chair.

7) Similarly, follow through on your promises so that they become effective incentives, and also so that your kids learn to keep their own promises.

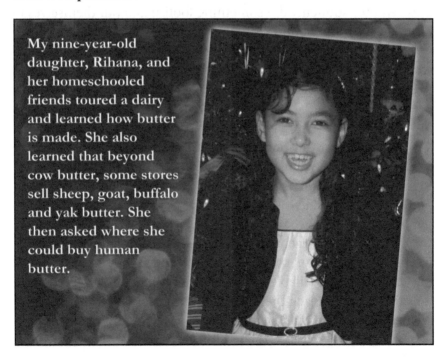

My nine-year-old daughter, Rihana, and her homeschooled friends toured a dairy and learned how butter is made. She also learned that beyond cow butter, some stores sell sheep, goat, buffalo and yak butter. She then asked where she could buy human butter.

8) Fight those early battles well: Parents are busy people and disciplining is often inconvenient. But, if you make a point of putting up with any inconvenience and addressing the issues early on, your kids will more quickly understand that they can not blackmail you with the inconvenience and you will endure far fewer interruptions, in the long run. Fail to do this and the smallest battles will rage on for years.

9) As long as your kids feel loved, safe and secure, the rest is much less important. The more love, safety and security you can provide, the less impact your parenting mistakes will have.

10) I'm not absolutely against spanking kids, but I have to mention that I've never had to do it in my eleven years as a parent. **If they are well loved, then a well-deserved spanking will not psychologically scar them.** However, as I believe they copy what we do, I can't really justify smacking a kid and then telling them not to hit others, or not to bully, because that's basically what a spanking is; conquering by force. The only times I've ever truly been tempted to smack my child was when he or she deliberately hurt my other child, or when they suddenly did something foolish and put themselves in harm's way. The reaction is instinctive, but I've managed to catch myself, just in time. I did, once, flick my son painfully on the shoulder when he recklessly endangered his little sister. It hurt his feelings more than his body, but I still feel guilty about this because of the look of betrayal he gave me.

11) Be fair in your punishments: If you punish too often, or are too heavy handed, you will be less effective. Especially in the heat of the moment, refrain from overreacting. I am slow to mete out punishment, usually starting with warnings, escalating to punishments if the behavior persists.

Early on, I had a theory that consequence would be a much better teacher than punishment. For example, if they broke a toy, then that toy would not be available to them and would not be replaced and I hoped this would teach them to care for their possessions. At first, it seemed to work. I could sit with a four-year-old and explain things like "if you don't go to sleep at bedtime, you will be tired the next day and might even get sick," and they seemed to get it and avoid the problem, in the future.

This idea worked really well until my kids were about eight. I guess that's when they realized that I was neither God nor Encyclopaedia Britannica and that the things I said might not be absolute truths. After that, they were not so easily persuaded by words and the idea of consequence. Instead, they began looking for ways to cheat the system. For instance, when my son got in the habit of chatting to his sister, keeping her awake long after bedtime. Reluctant to punish I just talked to him about it, the first few times. He lowered his voice to a whisper but continued. Finally, I revoked all of his computer privileges. Then he finally understood that I was serious and that there were consequences that mattered to him. That problem vanished.

12) Fairness and expectation: Kids—especially below the age of six—don't see unfairness the way adults do because they only have the expectations that we give them. For instance, my kids are often not allowed the same sugary/salty snacks as most of the other kids they play with. When they were very young, we told them that it was because we wanted them to be healthy, and we demonstrated our resolve by leaving events the first couple of times they made a fuss. These days, my kids are usually the only ones not hovering around the chip bowl and pestering their parents for more. And they do not feel cheated at all. Further demonstrating the point is the fact that the other kids quickly accepted that "normal" was the William M. Dean-kids having only 3-4 potato chips while everyone else filled a bowl.

13) Don't expect to be fair, all the time. Just because you eat cake does not mean that they get a piece, too. That's not how life works and anyway, ultimately, everything balances out because **every material thing you never got forced you to become a better person.** My sister has a little saying that she uses to cut short the whining: "Life's not fair, don't compare."

14) Be stingy with rewards but generous with praise. Try to find something positive to say about anything your child is proud of, but save high praise and rewards for when it's genuinely deserved. They will come to understand the difference and properly learn to evaluate their own efforts.

15) Lead by example: From what I've observed with friends and family, your daughter will tend to mimic her mother's behavior and your son will mimic his father's. It's obvious to us that my son takes after my wife's family, in body and brain, and yet, he thinks and behaves more like me. The exact opposite is true of my daughter.

16) Kids copy what you don't do, as well as what you do. I allow my kids to see stuff that includes foul language because trying to prevent exposure is impractical, but I do not swear. As a result, my kids know all the bad words and phrases, but they have never used them—yet.

17) Curse words: Don't worry about your kids hearing bad words. There is no way you can stop it and the lesson they really need to learn is not to repeat them. Bad words and most other taboos are completely arbitrary, but not respecting those taboos can affect your child's future, so they need to learn whom those words will offend and what the social consequences are.

After a home schooling pep talk...

"Actually, Dad, failure is an option."

18) Sexual content: Don't worry about them being accidentally exposed to sexual images. Kids only "see" what they understand. If what they see generates questions, then they are old enough to hear the answers. However, be careful to only answer what they specifically ask. Answer clinically and don't take things further unless prodded by another question. You might be surprised at how many obvious follow-up questions they don't ask.

19) Violent media: *Do* worry about exposing them to violent media—especially movies. This scares kids and makes them feel unsafe. Also, so much of what the media serves is unrealistically frequent and sadistic, which can skew their world-view.

20) Expectation, habit, comfort zones: One way to think about parenting is that you are instilling expectations, comfort zones and habits. An expectation might be "that you eat your vegetables because they are healthy." A good habit is something like brushing teeth. A comfort zone might be having a family reading time, just before bed. (Habits eventually become comfort zones, so the two are difficult—maybe impossible—to distinguish.)

21) No sugar before 5 years old: I read this somewhere and thought it might work, so we tried it with both our kids. They are now nine- and eleven-years old and both like sweets, but are very picky. They won't eat crappy store-bought birthday cake and don't care at all that every other kid at the party is chowing down. They also do not overindulge in sweets and never hover when junk food is put out. We monitor it minimally, but it takes them almost the entire year to eat their Halloween haul, and that's after they've given away everything they don't like. On the other hand, they must monitor me constantly to keep me away from their goodie bags because I'd lick sugar off a bee's bottom if I couldn't get it any other way.

22) Dental hygiene: Brush their teeth for them, at least twice a day, until they are five or six to make sure they develop the habit and learn how to do a good job. After that, they should brush after every meal and you will have to constantly check to make sure they are doing a good job. Electric toothbrushes have a built-in timer, which makes it easier to set a standard. Beyond brushing, we make our kids floss whenever they are watching TV, using the little plastic dental floss sticks, often called kid- or line-flossers. When it's not convenient to brush after a meal, we give our kids sugarless gum. We choose the adult-oriented mint-flavored ones because we don't want them to crave it enough to develop a gum-chewing habit. We also restrict this to no more than once a day. Neither of my kids has ever had a cavity.

23) Be conservative how much dental work is performed on your children. The best medicine is to not get sick. Everything else is a compromise. Make sure that your kids brush well and floss regularly. Have regular check-ups and cleanings. So many people have dental insurance through their jobs that it has become increasingly common that children have a lot of dental work done. Every filling they get will eventually weaken their teeth. When they are in their forty's and fifty's, this will start to become a problem. I'm proof of that. I haven't had a cavity in more than twenty years and yet the teeth that were filled in my childhood are slowly crumbling apart around the fillings, and there is nothing I can do to prevent it.

24) Be stingy with medicine. The rule that we have been able to adhere to for the past eleven years is that our kids only get medicine if a sickness is preventing them from eating or sleeping. Only once, at Christmas, did we ever dose one of our kids to get him through an event, and only then because he was almost over the illness. On top of this, we make sure they get plenty of sleep.

To fight fevers during the day, we've had good results from tepid baths. When their bodies are radiating heat, a tepid bath will feel uncomfortably cold, but we make them stay in at least five minutes and try to get them to fully immerse. If they can do fifteen minutes, the relief lasts longer—a couple of hours, with our kids.

We also give them homemade green tea popsicles which may help lower their fever, but certainly works as a distraction without introducing sugar, which I believe to be anti-medicine.

25) Children equate physical pain with emotional pain, or even just discomfort until they've gained enough experience to discriminate. At nine years old, my daughter is still unable to clearly distinguish many forms of discomfort from actual pain, which is sometimes panic inducing for me, when trying to diagnose a sickness or injury.

26) Kids need their sleep. It's important for their general health, and doubly important if they are sick. I put sleep at the top of the health pyramid, second only to air. Kids who get lots of sleep don't get sick as often and recover more quickly.

27) Bedtimes should be strictly enforced for the kids' good health, but also for the mental health of their parents. Every minute your children stay up past their bedtime eats into your recovery time. Tapped out adults cannot provide their children with the best care.

28) When they are babies, don't tiptoe around the house while they nap. **Make them bulletproof nappers.** The first few times it might seem crazy, but babies will sleep when they are tired, regardless of the circumstances so that's the best time to train them to ignore their surroundings. If your children are well trained to sleep you can enjoy a few hours of normal adult-time—have a heated discussion, entertain guests or watch a loud movie. Occasionally, my wife and I will turn on the light in their bedroom and have a short discussion, while watching them sleep.

NOTE: Napping during the day will only work when the kids need rest. Even as an infant, my son was simply never tired during the day and only slept at night. My daughter was the polar opposite, sleeping so much that I seriously considered seeking medical advice. I tried, but never found any way to change their natural sleeping patterns.

29) Let the baby cry. My initial theory was that if I rushed in every time the baby cried, he would learn that everything is ok and that he doesn't need to cry. In retrospect, this was a foolish notion. In fact, he learned to cry whenever he was not otherwise occupied. It took months to retrain both of us.

30) Self-esteem is trust in oneself. Like all trust, it cannot be gifted, but must be earned. Praise, alone, cannot build self-esteem. Only real accomplishments are confidence/self-esteem builders. **Encourage your kids to do stuff!** This is especially important for girls because our society emphasizes beauty over personality and integrity

while encouraging women to use their sexuality as social currency, all of which tends to undermine long-term self-esteem.

Self-esteem is trust in one's self.

Like all trust it must be earned.

This is why people who do things have higher self esteem

•

Get out there and do stuff!

31) Let them be bored. It teaches them to think and imagine and how to cope with boredom. It also makes chores and reading more attractive. Admittedly, this is a tough one for parents to endure because children tend to wander around pestering the adults when they are bored. I heard one parent tell her children: "Go outside and do something. You'll feel better about yourself." I thought it was very good advice because going outside is therapeutic and doing something—regardless how insignificant— contributes to self-esteem.

32) Hold your kids close whenever you can. Soon enough, they won't let you. Parenting is a never-ending process of letting go.

33) Spend time with them. One of the things they want more than anything else is time with their parents. You do not always have to come all the way down to their level or pay them full attention. My kids like playing in the yard while I'm gardening; happy to run and jump and come back to ask me questions or relate their observations about grass and bugs, every three or four seconds. It's not exactly adult-time but I do get to dig up some weeds and, occasionally, complete an entire thought.

For toddlers, a great summer idea I saw online was to **give them a paint bucket of water and a paintbrush and have them paint the fence with water!** Wet wood appears a different color than dry but, obviously, there is no clean up. Wish I'd thought of that one.

34) You can't pour tea from an empty cup. **Take care of yourself and your spouse first.** If you are completely drained, you will have

nothing to offer your children. Also, a lot of parenting is about letting go. As your kids get older, they will want their independence. In their twenty's, they probably won't be around much. Your spouse is your only constant companion in life. Take care of that relationship, not only is it your life preserver, it is, ultimately, the cruise ship you want to get back to.

35) Don't let kids get between you and your spouse. Kids are natural manipulators. And they start surprisingly early. When she was about four, my daughter tried to leverage a divide between my wife and I during an argument by asking me a pointed question the answer to which would likely have rekindled the debate, had we not recognized the manipulation attempt. At that time, my daughter viewed her mother as *"The Enforcer"* and me as *"Mr. Funtimes"* and was hoping to secure an ally in her minor disagreements with my wife. We presented a united front, saying that we do not agree on the topic, but that we did not expect to agree on everything, which seemed to put her in her place.

36) Stay together as long as possible. A reason for splitting up that is commonly deemed acceptable is that your unhappiness will affect the kids by showing them a bad model of marriage. Generally, I don't agree. Kids are basically all about themselves. They are barely aware that you and your wife *have* a relationship, let alone that it may be a bad one. All they really care about is stability and security and having love heaped upon them. If they had a vote, they would tell you to stay together and be miserable. From what I've seen, even an amicable divorce is a psychological ordeal for children that should be avoided, if at all possible.

37) Lie to your kids: We all lie to our kids about things like the Tooth Fairy, Easter Bunny and Santa Claus not for their benefit, but for our own. We want to foster those too-cute moments of magical wonder and drink them in like ambrosia. Ok—but you're really not doing your kids any favors by convincing them that magic exists, not to mention confusing the *"truth is always best"* message. As soon as they become sceptical, don't invest a lot of energy into prolonging the lie. If they ask the question, it is completely ok to tell them the answer, <u>provided they are old enough to keep a secret</u> from other kids because if they tell other kids who aren't ready—or, more likely, whose parents are not ready—you will probably find yourself in a heap of social trouble. If your kids can't be trusted with such a secret, lie your butt off or prepare to face the social consequences.

38) Teach them that taking responsibility earns privilege. All children should have chores. Start when they are very young, even though it will mean constant monitoring and reminding, because toddlers will accept work willingly. They have few expectations and a built-in urge to grow up, so they don't categorize tasks as "work" or "play." These chores should earn them trust, and privileges and lead to ever larger tasks. They also contribute to confidence and self-esteem.

39) Developmental Stages: It may drive you absolutely nuts, but while they are growing you will have to repeat the exact same things to them a million times until, magically, one day they seem to just suddenly "get it." It's not that they don't want to obey, it's that they can't.

My wife and I exhausted ourselves enforcing things like "no running in the house," "no yelling in the house," toilet training and putting away the toys. I especially remember the running thing, when my son was about four. He was very smart and unusually obedient but when I asked him to stop running, he'd take about three walking steps and then break into a run again, apparently having completely forgotten the entire encounter. Then one day, he just didn't run in the house anymore. I eventually concluded that their brains were just not able to process the instruction until that one certain brain cell was born and then, suddenly, they could.

I don't recall any such issues between six and ten years old, but now, at eleven, my son is suddenly overcome with energy, which he constantly vents as piercing vocalizations. He seems completely unaware that he's even being loud, so getting him to quiet down is a continuous effort. My wife and I are anxiously awaiting the birth of that new brain cell.

40) My daughter is a bit messy, constantly leaving her things all over the house. To help her see how this is inconvenient for the rest of us, I started referring to her as my "roommate." The roommate analogy seems to help her understand that we are equally sharing the common spaces and that it's unfair for one person to monopolize that space. It also makes her think about the future when she might actually be a roommate. **How to be a good roommate is a good concept to teach** because if they have abrasive and indulgent habits at home, they may be difficult for others to live with which will affect every future relationship, from roommate to life-partner.

41) Once they are old enough to care, **let them wear what they want** as long as it does not impact anyone but themselves. Going out on a winter day without a jacket will not make them sick; only germs can do that. However, they should be taught to be prepared. Leaving home without appropriate attire may put someone else at an inconvenience if the child becomes uncomfortable, or there is an unexpected emergency situation.

42) Instead of phrasing a question as yes/no, **presenting only acceptable options can avoid an unacceptable response.** For instance,

Instead of asking, "How much broccoli would you like?" try using "Would you like two pieces of broccoli, or four?" Your child will feel like he/she has made a choice and will be more likely to willingly accept the outcome.

43) My sister's tip: At large gatherings, kids often get involved in petty squabbles which can lead to a near-constant line of disgruntled young ones complaining to the adults. When kids report on other kids, one effective filter is to say: **"Is someone hurt? Is something broken? If not, then you are just tattling and we parents do not need to get involved."**

44) The Attitude Dance: *(Another of my sister's tips)* Whenever on of my sister's kids persisted with a bad attitude, she and/or their siblings might call out, "Attitude Dance!" at which point the offender had to dance while singing Patti LaBelle's *New Attitude* song, until they snapped out of it. It's completely silly and slightly embarrassing, but it works so well that most of the homeschoolers in our circles have adopted it. I will say that this is something that is best started young. Dealing with the embarrassment and learning humility are the core effects that make this effective, and it can be one of the tools you can employ to help bully-proof your kids.

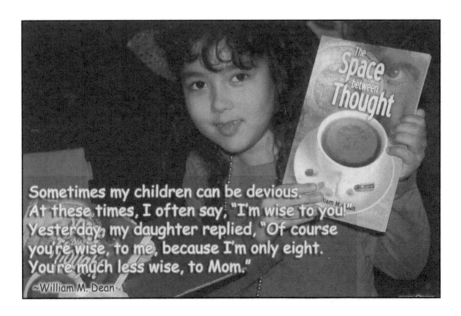

Sometimes my children can be devious. At these times, I often say, "I'm wise to you!" Yesterday, my daughter replied, "Of course you're wise, to me, because I'm only eight. You're much less wise, to Mom."
~William M. Dean

45) A friend of mine shared this trick for **getting a fussy baby to accept a soother:** if they spit it out, tap the end of it. They will instinctively clamp down and hold on to it, after that.

46) Another friend of mine makes her kids participate in the following conversation **whenever they whine about adults not following their own rules** she's made that they deem unfair...

Adult: What do kids do?
Kid (rolling eyes): What adults say.
Adult: And, what do adults do?
Kid (resigned sigh): Anything they want.
Oft-repeated phrases like this tend to cut short the whining.

Of course, reading 46 or even 46,000 parenting tips isn't going to make the job a breeze. I can only hope that you find some of these of such value that you name at least one of your children after me and mention me in your will. Anything beyond that may be asking too much.

27

Intimacy and Expectation

Because we are each unique, we each enter relationships with different expectations of intimacy.

If you find yourself constantly trying to get emotionally closer, but your partner seems to be doing everything in their power to sabotage your efforts, it could be that you are mismatched in your expectations. Conversely, the same may be true if you find your partner's attentions make you claustrophobic. Closing the gap in your expectations regarding intimacy is extremely important if you are to forge a lasting union.

Levels of Intimacy (Strong, Silent Type versus Stalker):

Everyone's comfort zone is different. Some people get uncomfortable if they are hugged. Others want to know their partner's every thought; aspiring to think and feel as one. There is no "correct" degree of intimacy, but if you are too unevenly matched, you will have your work cut out for you in bridging the gap. Intimacy-cravers will feel empty if coupled with stoic utilitarians, while strong-silent types will feel continually embarrassed and badgered by hopeless romantics.

If your partner's needs are too different from your own, it's difficult not to feel resentment at their efforts to get closer or to maintain emotional distance. Resentment needs to be resolved because it will damage you and your relationship. One way to dissolve resentment is to empathize with your partner by seeing their point of view. Try imagining those in other positions on the intimacy scale.

Let's say that you are a romantic expecting a high degree of emotional connection. In order to empathize with a reluctant partner, it's a good exercise to think about someone even higher on the scale than you. Imagine what they might demand of you, and how claustrophobic that could feel. That might be what your partner currently feels. And yet, no one is wrong. Your imaginary clingy-smotherer is not wrong for wanting to connect so closely. You are not wrong for feeling like you have a stalker and wanting a little more emotional space.

Similarly, your partner is not wrong for not shouting "I love you!" in Times Square, or for not kissing you in public.

No one is wrong. There is no more reason for them to change, than for you.

There is no reason for resentment.

However, the larger the intimacy gap, the more difficult the challenge of building a bridge.

Wandering Partners:

There are a lot of reasons why people cheat, but a common one would be to try to make up for an intimacy imbalance.

Sex is emotional candy. It can't sustain a full relationship but it's a boost to our self-esteem and provides an artificial feeling of intimacy. When there is an intimacy gap in a long-term relationship, there comes an urge to fill it. Sex is one easy way; though it's therapeutic affects are short term.

For some, a very low level of intimacy is their comfort zone. These people want this gap in their relationship yet still crave the feeling of closeness. For these people, the deep familiarity that comes with a long-term relationship can make them claustrophobic and a casual sexual partner can appear to be a very attractive option.

At the other end of the spectrum, intimacy-cravers need feedback from their spouse to maintain their self-esteem. A lack of communication can leave them feeling insecure and vulnerable to the attentions of another.

If you don't want your partner to cheat, or feel like cheating, you should do all you can to close the intimacy gap. But remember, this could just as likely mean allowing more emotional space, as it might mean deeply connecting. One, or both of you, may have to journey far beyond your emotional comfort zone.

5 Essential Elements

There are five basic elements necessary to create an environment in which intimacy may grow:

1) Trust: Trust cannot be given—it must be earned. When your partner earns your trust, it is important to recognize that fact by extending your trust. If your partner has never lied about anything important, they should be believed. If they have never cheated, they should have earned the right to not be accused without overwhelming evidence.

> ***A Note About Jealousy:**
> Acting on feelings of jealousy demonstrates a total lack of trust and is akin to nail-gunning your relationship's coffin. It's a defensive maneuver; an attempt to spare you from hurt feelings. It's as if the humiliation of being duped hurts worse than that of being dumped. This kind of pre-emptive strike is often a self-fulfilling prophecy. If your partner is

wandering, then this will certainly bring it into the open faster. But if they aren't, then your unwarranted jealousy is guaranteed to drive them away. An innocent person will be offended that their good behavior has earned them so little trust. It will certainly impair the bonds of intimacy.

One thing that can help is to cut your partner some slack. Be slow to accuse and quick to forgive. Accept that everyone examines their options. Everyone looks at attractive people and wonders what it would be like to be with them. Everyone is tempted, at some time or other. Be honest with yourself. Has your eye never wandered? If you don't consider yourself a cheater, then don't accuse your partner just because someone caught their eye.

Some are driven to jealous accusations by fears that they might appear foolish to their friends. But being a raging paranoid reveals much more weakness than being a trusting dupe. Having your trust abused is not a bad reflection on you.

If you don't trust, you can't be scammed, but then neither can you achieve intimacy.

2) Trustworthiness: Earning your partner's trust is the flip side of the deal. Since it takes two to create intimacy, you must give your partner good reason to trust you.

3) Honesty: Be honest with your partner. In order to do this, you really must be honest with yourself.

4) Caring: You must care about your partner. Regardless of your differences and disagreements, you must be looking out for your partner's well being, though not at the expense of your own.

5) Acceptance: You must accept differences of opinion, nature, mood, logic, and behavior. Your partner will never become your twin. That's a good thing. You are not the lexicon of proper human behavior: There is no such thing. Allow for idiosyncrasies. Learn to step back. Shake your head, maybe, but learn to laugh.

A strong commitment is a big help with all of this. Believing that you will be together at the end of any incident will help keep your behavior and your responses to your partner's behavior, within bounds. In the end, whether or not you manage to cement your relationship really depends upon which is larger; your motivation or the intimacy gap.

Before you speak,
ask yourself:

Is it kind,
is it true,
is it necessary,
does it improve
upon the silence?

~Shirdi Sai Baba

Not So Hardcore

28

Fitness Core Concepts for the rest of us

The other day, I surprised a beautiful woman in the shower and she complimented me by calling me "hardcore"—and she wasn't referring to how much junk food I can consume, which was a nice change. Putting this in context: she's the cleaning lady at my gym and this exchange took place while she was refilling the soap dispensers. For almost five years, I've watched her roam about making everything shiny and smell like flowers but this was the first time we'd really talked.

My take away from fifteen minutes of conversation was that she is as sweet as she looks and that she called me "hardcore!" I'd never felt more macho.

The sad truth, though, is that I'm not hardcore at all. I work out, for about an hour, three times a week. The guys who come in at six a.m., heft my body weight in metal for two hours, and have been doing so every day since they were eighteen; *they* are hardcore!

I'm no jock and I dislike almost every minute of my workout, but I'm in my mid-fifties and had kids late in life, so I truly believe that I need to keep fit in order to remain healthy enough, long enough to escort my kids into adulthood and then to enjoy retirement. Why I think I'll need muscles to lie in a hammock on a tropical beach sipping Corona, I'm not sure. Maybe it's because, despite my best efforts, there is little evidence that my retirement will include hammocks on tropical beaches and a lot of evidence suggesting I might be working until I die. I'm pretty confident, though, that beer will figure in.

I think and write a lot and, consequently, lead a largely sedentary life. I'm so much in my own mind that actually *doing* things feels like a rude interruption. My relatively intense one hour at the gym keeps me fit and gives me a break from a never-ending barrage of thoughts; like a relief valve for my psyche—sorely needed, because sometimes I get bored of my own voice inside my head: It's nasally and judgmental.

I decided to shed my pudgy executive body and lifestyle about twenty-five years ago, and since that time I've made a concerted effort to stay active. For the past ten years, I've been working out regularly. Along the way, I've learned a few very basic things, which I'd like to share. Many of these things might seem obvious, but almost every day I witness newcomers wasting time and effort and needlessly torturing themselves in misguided efforts at getting into shape. When you don't have the proper expectations, regime or technique, the results are discouraging and, eventually, you don't do it at all. Which is the worst outcome possible.

What follows are ten core concepts that I have discovered. These apply to all of us less-than-elite athletes and are the essential ideas that keep me safe and fit and—most importantly—keep me coming back to the gym.

1) The Most Basic Question—Why?:

My grandmother was a crafty old lady who never shied away from a good lie if it would get her what she wanted. In order to make sure the grandkids turned the taps off, she told us that water was five cents a drop. You never think to question things your grandmother tells you and, one day when I was twenty-four and in a business meeting, the topic of water bills came up. I hadn't yet bought a house and had never had a water bill of my own, but I commiserated by telling the others that I was sympathetic, considering that water cost five cents a drop. Suddenly, all conversation stopped and every head turned my way. It was not the kind of limelight I had been seeking. Then someone did some quick math to set me straight while I turned fifty shades of red.

When she was about eighty-five, well after my grandfather had passed, she started dating but didn't like confrontation. When she wanted to dump a boyfriend, she told them that she was a secret agent and had to leave the country and change her identity. They either bought the story or got the message—I don't think she cared which, just so long as they left her alone.

She was full of energy and had always looked much younger than her age, so because she wanted to work ten years past the usual retirement age, she knocked ten years off her age and told everyone her birth certificate had been destroyed in a fire. Consequently, when she died, no one knew her exact age. By our family's best reckoning, she was either ninety-four or ninety-eight.

She taught me a lot of things—some even turned out to be true! But the most important truth was to come at her expense.

She was unusually fit and active and no one I ever met who was her age could ever keep up. But then, one day, she fell. She would have been about ninety, at that point. The fall broke some ribs, and glass from a cabinet she fell against tore a large hole in her thigh. She was stitched back together but, probably based on her age, the Doctor told her to rest for at least three months. And that was the beginning of the end. She never really got back out of the chair she was forced to sit in for months. She had a sharp mind until very near the end, but she certainly lost the majority of her vitality in one fell swoop.

That her recovery was so much less than total startled all of us. And for me, it graphically demonstrated an old Chinese proverb: *The best cure is: don't get sick.*

Aging has reinforced this lesson. I rarely have any aches or pains but I notice that those around me started having chronic complaints soon after reaching forty. When I'm among a crowd that is over fifty, I am usually the only one not complaining about some physical discomfort, or talking about medical procedures and pharmaceuticals.

The only discernable difference between me and most of my friends is that I have tried to balance my sedentary work life with regular exercise. If you sit at a desk all day, like most of us, you need to counter the negative effect on your body or else you will slowly incur injury. Once you are injured, you must rely on your body's recuperative powers to restore balance. The effectiveness of this strategy diminishes as we age. If that doesn't work, you will need assistance from the medical system. Once you are at that point, restoring balance becomes even more difficult because all medicines have side effects. Sometimes, the side effects seem minimal, but eventually, they cause injury; and the spiral tightens.

2) Workouts vs. Diets:

Nothing you do at the gym can control your weight. Don't start with the goal of reducing your weight. Only dieting can do that. The body is so efficient that you could strenuously lift weights for an hour without losing a single pound that you wouldn't later gain back. To give you some perspective: I use the treadmill or stationary cycle for 18 minutes and according to the display panels, I burn about 250-275 calories. It's a rigorous workout for me and by the end, I'm half-drenched in sweat. One can of fruit juice is 140-160 calories; a chocolate bar; close to 300. A large coffee with cream and sugar is 280 calories!

That walk from your car to the office, up the stairs, swiveling about in your cubicle, then back to your car, up your front stairs, turning the key in the lock, plus stooping to retrieve the newspaper and later lifting yourself out of your recliner and the ten steps to the fridge and back—your entire physical day—would probably consume less than 100 calories. The average person burns the majority of calories through nervous energy and body heat. There is just no practical way to burn off excess fat by working out.

What exercise will do for you is convert fat to muscle. So if you are happy with your weight, you can alter your shape into something healthier and more attractive.

If you are unhappy with your weight, reduce your food intake.

3) Go Often:

The easiest way to commit to a gym is to focus on the long-term goal of extending and improving your life and to consider the gym membership a lifestyle choice rather than a quick means to a short-term end. Getting in shape for bikini season, or your grad reunion, probably won't work as well as you hope and will not be motivation enough to keep you attending the gym once your goal date passes.

To stay in shape, especially as you age, you will need to exercise on a regular basis. So don't try a routine that is so harsh that you dread it. You're far better off to step it down a few notches so that you look forward to the workout. Twenty minutes of moderate exercise every day will contribute more to your long-term health than a rigorous one-hour workout, three times a week. And, of course, it's better than a workout so onerous that you never do it.

4) Stressors:

Nowhere is it so apparent that mental and physical health are connected than at the gym. After five years, my muscles are used to my workout and there is no doubt that I can perform the same series any day of the week. However, sometimes I just don't have the mental energy required to ignore the fatigue. On those days, I may have to break a set into smaller portions or lower the weight. It's always disappointing, especially as I know that it's entirely mental. What's happening is that I am reaching my maximum stress load.

Stress is part of life. And the right amount of stress is a good thing. It keeps us motivated and focused and helps us achieve things. But there is a limit to how much stress an individual can endure without it having a negative impact. Exercise is a stressor, and a strenuous workout does not always relieve stress—it can add to it. Take note of your accumulated stresses from things like maintaining relationships, your job, health issues, frantic schedules, and financial issues. If some of them are peaking, then don't worry if you have to lower your load at the gym. Continually powering through may add unmanageable stress to your life, which may damage more than it heals.

Stubbornly sapping your mental and physical energy may ultimately put your gym routine at risk. Above all, the goal is to continue going.

5) Cardio is Number One:

I'd guess that at least two-thirds of the good in my regime comes from the cardio: treadmill/cycles. If you can't make yourself do anything else, do this. Fifteen minutes on one of these machines will make the largest difference to the quality of your life, as well as life expectancy.

If you've ever seen charts showing the leading causes of death as we age, you may have noticed that the largest killers, after the age of 65, are respiratory- and circulatory-related: the result of what we've done to ourselves. As we age—and as the price of Netflix drops—we tend to become more sedentary. This results in shallower breathing, a slowed heart rate and reduced circulation. The arteries harden, all the related essential muscles weaken and, eventually, something fails. Cardio exercise keeps your lung-expanding muscles in shape, which deepens your breathing. It also moves the blood through your system which feeds the tissues, scrubs the artery walls, purifies the blood, and exercises your most important muscle group; the heart.

The theory I'm going with—and this is entirely my own perspective—is that if everything is in good running order then when something finally fails it will have racked up the maximum mileage and then, either things will be repairable because the rest of me is healthy enough to withstand the procedure or the end will be quick. The one outcome I hope to avoid is slowly and painfully fading away. Odds are, my mind will be the first to go and none of this will matter.

6) Weights vs. Cardio:
While lifting weights, take lots of breaks and do not allow yourself to feel short of breath. Weight lifting is for mobility-muscle building, not for cardio. Being short of breath will just make it more painful and will not build any of the larger muscle you were hoping for. In fact, if you exhaust yourself during weights, you will tend to get sloppy in performing the exercise, thus reducing the benefit. Leave the heavy breathing for the cardio portion of the routine.

7) Reps vs. Weight:
Heavier weights build more muscle. Lower weights are less likely to cause injury. Find the balance that works for you.

Lifting a total of 300 lbs. by doing 100 reps of 3 lbs., is the same amount of work as doing 10 reps of 30 lbs., but less likely to cause injury. But, though the lower weight/higher reps contribute 300 lbs.-

worth of fitness to your body, it will not result in large muscles that show. To gain showy muscle, as you get more fit slowly increase the weight and decrease the reps accordingly, making sure to calculate that you are doing the same total amount of work, or more. As your weights increase and the reps decrease, muscle growth will become more obvious.

I am very cautious in increasing weight because it's better to proceed slowly but steadily than to have to take a week off to nurse an injury. In the regime I follow, I mostly do 45 reps of each exercise. To increase the load, I usually start by doing only 15 of the 45 reps at a greater weight. I continue this for two weeks to a month. Then I step up to 30 reps with increased weight. A month later, that entire exercise is done at the new, higher weight.

I don't rush because I have no short-term goals: This is for life, in every sense of the phrase.

8) Controlled Motion:

Do not allow yourself to rely on momentum when lifting weights. Don't let the weights swing loosely; always make the movements slow and controlled. Otherwise, you are "cheating" and not getting the best workout. By taking advantage of momentum you might actually avoid using the muscles which most need the workout and for which that exercise was intended. Better to do fewer reps perfectly than more reps sloppily because that is just a waste of time and the lack of results may be discouraging.

Also, be conscious of your posture. Keeping everything straight and un-hunched will help isolate the muscles you are working on, as well as giving smaller support muscles a workout.

9) Injuries:

The two most common injuries are stiff muscles and pulled muscles. You need to recognize the difference and treat them accordingly.

- **Stiff muscles:** This is due to a build-up of lactic acid in your muscles and the best way to shorten the suffering is to keep moving. Continue your exercise routine, but reduce the load a bit so that you are not exacerbating the problem. As you move the blood, your organs remove the excess acid and relieve your pain. Resting also works, but is slower and, of course, allows your conditioning to slide.

• **Pulled Muscles:** A pulled/torn or overextended muscle will often feel as if you could sort it out just by stretching more. Do not stretch these injuries. Instead, leave them alone and rest. You can still exercise, but avoid using that group of muscles.

To aid in healing, applying cold and heat alternately at 15-minute intervals is very good therapy. The cold reduces internal swelling while the heat encourages blood flow to deliver healing nutrients and remove damaged cells.

I'm not one to pop a pill, but occasionally, when there seems no way to relieve a sore spot (especially in my back) I have found it helpful to take an anti-inflammatory drug like Advil, Aleve or aspirin because some injuries take place in spots that are continually in use which exacerbates the condition. Chemically reducing the swelling can give relief to the problem and allow the healing to start.

10) Hire a Professional Trainer:

I'm simply too cheap to pay to have a personal trainer continually at my side. And I'm not sure what this constant coaching achieves. It seems to me that after a few sessions, once you've got the routine down, they are little more than highly paid cheerleaders. I prefer to do some work, achieve some results then go back for a session in which they watch me and critique my technique or tweak the program.

However, when first starting out, I definitely recommend you hire a professional trainer for a session or two in order to establish a safe and effective exercise regime. Most gyms will be able to recommend a trainer. All the ones I've encountered have given me great advice. I am still working on a routine given to me four years ago. I've made slight alterations and increased my weights, but it is essentially unchanged. A great value, and something I'd consider essential.

My Routine:

I make it to the gym about three times a week, consistently. My routine is made up of four different sets of three exercises (tri-sets). I do two of the four, plus 18 minutes of treadmill or cycle each day. I'm no Adonis, but this keeps me fitter than most men, and as I age, the difference between sedentary individuals and us exercisers becomes more obvious.

• **Warm-up Stretches:**

I do a few basic stretches just to limber up. I stretch areas that are prone to damage. This will be different for each person. I made up my own stretch routine and none of the trainers ever thought it was important enough to alter. For a long time, I did 15 minutes of stretching but found the benefits to be minimal. Now I'm down to about 3 minutes.

One note of caution: do not over-stretch. Consider cold muscles to be elastic bands taken directly from a deep freezer. If you fully extend a frozen elastic, it will snap. Cold muscles are prone to similar damage: they may tear. More worrisome yet: you probably won't feel it during your exercise because of the endorphins flooding your system. The injuries that have kept me away from the gym the most have been from overextending.

***Note:** You can find pictures
of all of the exercises mentioned below
by typing the exact names into a search engine.*

• **Tri-set #1**

Mountain Climb (3 x 15): Set yourself up in a stance as if you were about to start the 100-yard dash in the Olympics, then jump slightly and shift your front foot to the rear and your rear one to the front, as if you were actually running. Repeat as fast as you can. This is a cardio exercise used to keep your heartbeat high which I'm told maximizes the effectiveness of the other exercises.

Incline Dumbbell Press (3 x 15): Lie on a bench, flat on your back. Use a comfortable dumbbell weight, one in each hand. Your arms should be perpendicular to your body, elbows bent so that the weights are even with your body. Lift the weights up by straightening your arms upwards, then down.

Seated Cable Row (3 x 15): Use the machine that has a seat close to the ground and allows you to pull weight toward your chest, as if you are rowing. Try to keep your back straight, and try not to hunch your shoulders.

• **Tri-set #2:**

Dumbbell Squats (1 x 20 reps): squat while holding small (5 lb. to start) dumbbells in each hand. Keep your back straight and go as low as you can.

Walking Lunge (2 x 15 reps): Extended stride that will take our butt down to knee level. Leg forward until knee joint is at 90 degrees. Then lift to standing and repeat stepping forward with your other leg. Move forward one step at a time in this fashion. Once you've mastered this one, you can add hand weights.

Hamstring Curls (1 x 20 reps): Lie on your back with a large rubber ball under your heels. Lift your body until you are straight as a board. Then, bend your knees, rolling the ball under your feet and in toward your butt.

• **Tri-Set #3:**

Double Crunch (3 x 15): Lying down flat on your back, fists against each temple, body curled so that your knees are at bent at 90 degrees. Then use your stomach muscles to curl yourself so that your elbows touch your knees. Make sure to keep your knees as close to 90 degrees as possible. Be careful when you first try this one as you can easily bruise your stomach muscles without knowing it. I'd suggest trying two sets of ten and build toward the full set of 45 reps.

Seated Dumbbell Shoulder Press (3 x 15): Sit on a chair-like bench with a weight in each hand, your elbows bent, so the weights are near shoulder level; as if you were Superman, lifting a car. Straighten your arms upward, then back down to shoulder height.

Lat. Pull Down (3 x 10): Find the machine that has a large metal bar hanging from it and a seat for you to sit on: you will be facing the machine. Set the weight where you want it and pull that bar down to nipple height. Keep your back straight and try not to hunch your shoulders.

• **Tri-Set #4:**

Burpee (1 x 15): Start in a standing position. Fall into a pushup position, keeping your body as rigid and straight as possible. Then jump back up to standing. Do this 15 times. You'll be surprised how winded you will get. This is a cardio exercise.

Dumbbell curls (3 x 15): One small dumbbell in each hand, arms hanging at your sides. Bend your elbows to bring the dumbbells to shoulder height, then back down. For best balance, alternate arms. If you alternate, then two curls counts as one.

Tri-cable Press Down (3 x 15): Find a machine that you can stand at, but has a short metal bar that allows you to pull the weight straight downward. Place your hands on the bar so that they are in line with your shoulder. Pull down, as far as you can, keeping your back straight and do not hunch your shoulders. Generally it is not wise to lock your joints during exercises, but this is one in which I would suggest you lock your elbows at full extension to get the maximum benefit.

I only do two of the above Tri-Sets each day. Then I head to the treadmill or stationary cycle and set it for a 18-minute program of hills. From start to finish, this routine take me about an hour. Then I hit the showers.

Then I go grab a donut, coke float and side of fries because that's the area in which I truly am hardcore.

My preferred stance when heading for the fridge.

29

Buying Out of Selling

Scouting Journal:
Day 5, Lake District Campaign
This may prove to be my final entry. Fiscal year end draws near, and I am frought with worry. Mayfield, Vargis and Dad report grave losses, in the field. Our investment in popcorn scented candles and bubble-gum pot pourri, though inspired, may prove our undoing...
Profits are down.
All seems lost.

I've always thought that the idea of fundraising for kids' activities was deeply flawed. Your kid sells something I don't really want to me, then my kid sells something useless to you. In the end, how is this better than me funding my own child, and you funding yours? Of course, your parents are also dragged into this—but really, they gave you life, food and shelter for twenty years. Was that not enough?

Moreover, why does learning to play the trombone, or sail, or camp in the woods necessitate our children working as slave labor, in retail sales? We send our kids to scouts to learn about the outdoors, not to end up hawking third-party goods that few people really want.

It's brilliant marketing, though; cute kids going door to door. It'd be hard to come up with anything more effective, short of Playboy

Bunnies shucking in male locker rooms. *(What? I said, "shucking.")* But, unless they're selling copies of my books, I'm against it.

These days, a lot of parents' free time is more valuable than their money. So, rather than insisting that kids (parents, really) sell, relative-to-relative, friend-to-friend and door-to-door, volunteer organizations should not overlook offering an option to "buy out of selling"—a lump-sum payment, in lieu of participation. Not having to cover the cost of third-party merchandise will make this more affordable.

After all, the primary goal is to generate money in order to provide the kids a better experience, not indoctrinate them in capitalism and corporate greed.

This is the type of form I would like my kids to bring home.

Thank you, in advance, for your support!

$15: I do not want to bake, so here is the money I would have spent on those cupcakes.

$25: I do not want to hit up my friends, family and co-workers, so here is the money I would have spent buying wrapping paper.

$50: I do not want to walk, swim, or run in any activity that has the word "thon" in it. Here is the money I would have spent on my child's "free" t-shirt.

$100: I really wouldn't have helped anyway, so here is $100 to forget my name.

$___ I am making this donation to express my appreciation for having nothing to buy, or do except fill out this form.

What Life Looks Like

Recently, I visited with someone I hadn't seen in about twenty years, except on Facebook. Let's call her Phoenix, because that would be cool if her name was Phoenix. Though we have very little in common, Facebook decided that I would be fascinated by the details of her life as a hobby farmer and organic activist and that I needed to see everything she ever posted, everyday, in my newsfeed. I did not agree, but Facebook took care of all the details and maintained the connection for me and I was too lazy to alter these settings.

About a year ago, I noticed some very interesting things begin to happen in her posts. She seemed to have acquired religion—and not one of the many mainstream ones—this one involved rainbows, crystals, auras and past lives. The change seemed to happen rapidly and I could tell that she was in very deep. And then, out of the blue, she messaged me and I felt inspired to meet with her.

Why? Well, firstly, I always felt that she was an interesting person and I do care about her. I actually care about pretty much every person I ever met—especially if they are attractive and female.

Admittedly, I have trouble letting go of friendships, and even casual acquaintances. Before Facebook, I would go to great lengths to maintain relationships with people who would otherwise have been naturally selected out of my day-to-day existence. The closest I come to understanding this compulsion is that either I am afraid that one of these connections will prove valuable beyond reason or I am afraid of losing the entertainment value of the people in my life. It's truly mystifying to me because I'm also terrified of being caught in obligations that eat up valuable me-time, like helping someone else move *(FYI: everyone I move appears to be a reckless hoarder to me, while I'm doing it)*, or shooting their wedding video *(I'll likely title it "Angela's First Wedding," because I'm a cynic)* or having to make a speech at their kid's graduation from reform school *(opening line: As we stand here, today, congratulating Brad on his early release, I can't help but think that one of his buddies is currently breaking into my house...")*.

Probably the largest reason I wanted to meet with Phoenix was that I was curious how this drastic change in belief systems had affected her marriage and friendships. Also, I hadn't written in a while and may have been hoping for new material—which, it turns out, I got.

I am always interested in alternate points of view. In particular, I am curious how beliefs that are very far from my own survive the tests of everyday observation and reality. For instance, if you believe that you can telekinetically summon a protective force field, then how do you reconcile that with the fact that the rock I just threw hit you in the head and that we are now in an ambulance on the way to a hospital? By the way, sorry about that, I guess I didn't have to pick such a large one, or throw it so hard, but on the other hand it shows how much I believed in you. That *is* a nasty dent, but you're insured, right? Oh, and what were you planning to say to the police?

Anyway, I met Phoenix for lunch and, as I'd guessed, her entire life was in upheaval but her new-found religion was keeping her eerily calm and composed. Her husband had left her, neglecting to take his debts with him. She was forced to sell her house and was moving her few remaining possessions into a storage locker, this made more difficult by the fact that no longer had a car. She was soon to start living out of a backpack and showering at a local campsite. But, she seemed completely at peace.

In fact, she seemed to be vibrating with excitement and positive energy. If I had been her, I would have been despondent and desperate and drinking heavily—possibly sniffing kerosene in a ditch along the side of the highway while trying to calculate whether my body was worth more being prostituted or parted out to science; though the answer to that is not really in doubt.

Beyond the obvious physical realities of her life, which were astounding in their own right, the things that were happening in her mind were also incredible. She had recently remembered an entire history of past lives and had connected, via the Internet, with others who had been part of her past, including several husbands. She explained to me that she had also recently become "fully psychic" and thus could now instantly distinguish between good and evil people. Throughout our visit her eyes would briefly glaze over as she broke away to commune with distant friends and ancient relatives, like a teenager ignoring you to text.

Talking with her was absolutely fascinating and I had a good time, but at one point I had to ask her to slow down because her world and mine are so disparate that I felt like I was translating every phrase from one language to another and it was exhausting.

I think that we both enjoyed ourselves, but it felt a bit as if we'd chatted on the Hypernet, met on Earth for a speed-date that didn't prove a match and then both happily returned to our home worlds understanding that I was Martian and she was, at the very least Venusian, possibly Plutonian and that this could never work, long term.

A couple of weeks later, while having tea with my Mom and Dad, I recounted this meeting. My Mother and I are similar in nature and she instantly understood my curiosity and how I could suspend my skepticism, going in. My Father, on the other hand, thought my friend was a "nutbar," and me as well for getting within a hundred feet of her. He asked me how I could understand a single word she said and whether I bought into any of it. I told him that I had to translate things like "energies," "auras," "angels," "devils," and "past lives" into terms that I could relate to in my world, but that I didn't reject her interpretation.

My Father would probably call himself a straight shooter; a simple man who sees things as they *really* are. He said, "That's just a bunch of mumbo-jumbo, psycho crap." I tried to explain to him my personal "model of Life," a visual aid I use to understand how someone else's view of the world can be so extremely different from my own. Imagine that everyone in the universe is standing in a large circle, jammed shoulder to shoulder as close as they can get. Now imagine that at the center of the circle is an object. It is very large, three-dimensional and complex. A person standing on the opposite side of the object sees an entirely different shape, texture and colour, and cannot see through it enough to see his opposite member. That object is Life.

In the circle, a person very close to you shares common experiences of things like culture, schooling and heritage. As they are looking from a point of view extremely close to yours they have a very similar perspective on Life, and therefore they see it much the way you do. Those further away get an entirely different view of life and are, therefore, less like you.

A person on the opposite side of Life is looking at the same object but seeing something entirely different. Because Life is so large and not transparent, this person is unable to even see you, let alone understand you. To such a person, you and your core values are all vaguely imaginable fantasy.

In my model, no one's view is exactly the same. No one's view is the whole picture. All views are valid.

This is how I can understand and accept experiences as radically different from mine as my friend, Phoenix's, with out threatening my own beliefs in any way. In the final analysis, all I am really concerned about is whether this alternate point of view might be destructive to the person, or to those around them.

There was a pregnant pause while my Father stared at me, over the top of his newspaper. My guess is that he was trying to decide if I was really his kid. I sometimes forget that not everyone needs to construct a visual aid to navigate Life. My father is a prime example. I think that he's an extremely happy man, but he has no built-in desire to dissect his universe. He is a doer, not a ponderer. He thoroughly enjoys playing golf and Internet poker, watching movies and socializing with family and friends. Beyond that, he has little interest. There are distinct advantages to being this way, the primary one being that he is almost perpetually satisfied with life—so long as Netflix runs smoothly. As well, he tends not to hand out a lot of unsolicited advice. This could be wisdom in action. Or, it could be that he doesn't have any advice. These things make him an attractive person and fun to be with. On the other hand, he is quick to tell you how wrong you were, after the fact, which can make him much less fun to be with, but fulfills him as a parent. So, again, he's happy.

"You're as crazy as she is," he declared, shaking the wrinkles out of the broadsheet and retreating to the safety of rational things like religious extremists, genocide, rape and murder.

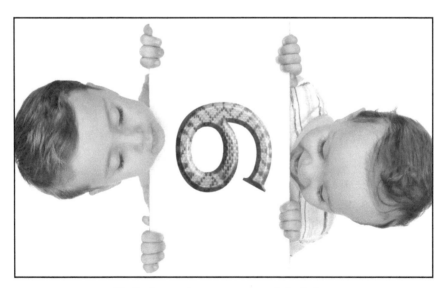

Truth depends upon your point of view.

31

Overdeveloped
Nations

Everyone loves Disneyland, and it's not difficult to understand why. Disneyland is an idealized, amplified reality offering sanitized fun and excitement, with all the danger removed. It's life-candy. And who doesn't love candy?

Recently, I was standing in line for the gondola ride at Disney Sea, in Tokyo, and noticed a lone duck casually swimming about in the canal. It struck me that I had rarely seen a duck unaccompanied by a flock. So why was this one alone? Because, in Disneyland, a wild duck is a contaminant. Disneyland is a completely controlled environment and so, to the caretakers at Disneyland, that duck must represent potential chaos and will surely be "taken care of" the moment it is not in public view. I checked the high windows and didn't see any snipers, but that doesn't mean they weren't there.

I can relate. I know how difficult it is to control my own little patch of Earth. I have to maintain a relatively dead, foot-wide gravel space around my house in order to deter pests. Once a year, I spray insecticide all the way around. Every year or two, I cut and haul away encroaching tree limbs, to prevent their leaves fouling the gutters, and I am constantly pulling up Ivy and Morning Glory to keep them from twining their way under the siding. The house itself has been constructed from lumber infused with anti-mold, water-resistant chemicals and all the concrete has been sealed to repel water. This, and constant vigilance, is what it takes to encourage some flowery bits of nature while keeping all of the rest at bay, for a single dwelling. Imagine what must be involved to secure an entire theme park. And, Disneyland does more than keep nature at bay. It eliminates it entirely, then reimagines, reengineers and reproduces it in sterile plastic or tightly controlled environments. Imagine the lengths they have to go to in their semi-tropical, coastal locations to deter such things as seagulls, crows, ants, spiders, ducks, mold and mildew.

There are more little brown birds at a single McDonald's, than I saw in all of Disney Sea. Canals and artificial lakes surrounded by food vendors coupled with the absence of mice, rats, mosquitoes, ants and houseflies implies the heavy use of pesticides and insecticides. Fabulous, continually blooming gardens devoid of weeds means fertilizers, herbicides and more insecticides. It's impossible for this to exist, otherwise.

I still love Disneyland and am filled with awe at its perfection, and gratitude for the experience. But, because I have to wait in line with my mind idly spinning, and because I am who I am, the hidden costs and implications of the theme park cascade, even as I am smiling.

(Note to Disneyland Execs: long waits in line
encourage authors to overthink.
It might be best to automatically move
all writers and their entourage to the head of the line.)

Most view Disneyland is an icon of happiness. But, really, it is the icon for the first-world pursuit of happiness. As we lose natural relaxers such as free time, elbow room and nature, we manufacture intensified, amplified versions to make up for it. Disneyland jams artificial, exaggerated landscapes into a space a tenth the size of it's parking lot in order to help the beleaguered, misguided millions get away from the very life they are clamoring to create. Similarly, indoor water parks offer artificial beaches, eternal sunshine, moderated surf, designer palm trees and ant-free concessions. Again, jamming what was once commonplace and accessible into minimal space, sanitizing the experience and charging people money—the physical manifestation of time spent doing something they *don't* want to do—for time spent doing something fun, in the hope of achieving some balance.

Of course, we have always been involved in this trade off. Millions of years ago, our ancestors struggled just to survive. Eventually, we became so proficient at survival that we gained some free time. We've been busy generating free time, ever since. But free time, is not free. A hundred years ago, one hour of free time might have cost fourteen

Disney Sea in Tokyo, Japan. The world's most enchanting ecological scar.

hours of farm labor. With the invention of machines and factories, the cost seemed to plummet. But it didn't, really. It just seemed that way because the planet Earth began to subsidize our project.

Earth has been so generous, that we have come to regard "free time" as being truly free. It's not, and we need to become more sensitive to the costs, or risk blindly working longer for all of those "labor-saving" devices, rather than working less *because* of them. Due to our lack of foresight, the machines are taking control, and without the aid of anything as sophisticated as Skynet.

The most obvious example is the automobile. Think of the effort and expense that has gone in to paving twelve billion miles (19 billion km) of roadway through mountains and forests, building bridges, tunnels and large ferries and then allocating space for parking—at home, as well as at every possible destination—just so that every single one of us can travel where we want, whenever we want. The enormity of this undertaking is difficult to imagine. And, beyond the cost of our vehicles, we continue paying for the entire infrastructure, every time we make a purchase or pay taxes. Add to this the environmental impact of manufacturing a vehicle with all it's exotic, high-tech components, then multiply that by the billion units made, so far, and the impact of this single device on the Earth can't be anything short of devastating.

We thought that things like cars could save us from drudgery. But, actually, factories, farms and governments did that, reducing the cost of survival to the point where, each day, we now trudge to work and do stuff we don't want to do, mostly in order to purchase more toys. Then, at the end of the workday, we crash in front of the TV thinking, "I'm too tired to vacuum." Which leads someone to invent a robot vacuum. And the circle tightens.

I'm not saying that we have to take a step backward. It's too late for that. But we should take a careful look at this mindless urge to push "forward," manufacturing ever more unsustainable comfort zones.

It's a kind of religion, the belief that technology will be our savior; no less than a belief in divine intervention. And it fuels a crusade to race pell-mell into the future, process the world and remake it in a form custom tailored for the human race.

We often hear about the plight of underdeveloped nations, but a larger problem is overdeveloped nations pushing to build bigger, better, faster progress-treadmills, and with obsessive-compulsive zeal.

Developed nations are missionaries to underdeveloped nations. But, along with aid, they serve a message of technological salvation: Selling the idea that progress is, in fact, progress.

The reality may be more that misery loves company.

Addendum:

I don't mean to rain all over Mickey's parade. In fact, my minimal research shows that Disney is conscious of all of the issues associated with its theme parks and has made many innovative changes designed to minimize its ecological impact. Still, its environmental impact remains enormous.

Related articles...

What is the Ecological Footprint of Disneyland?
by David Ng (May 5, 2009)
http://scienceblogs.com/worldsfair/2009/05/05/what-is-the-ecological-footpri-1/

Fallout Over Disneyland
by Amy Davis and Gar Smith
http://www.earthisland.org/journal/index.php/eij/article/fallout_over_disneyland/

Arguments: 10 Rules of Engagement

Arguing is an unavoidable part of the process of forging an intimate relationship.

A good argument is some combination of two things:

a) negotiating for things you want,

b) attempting to better understand an event or behavior.

To minimize the bloodshed, it's a good idea if you can agree on some rules of engagement. Here are my suggestions...

1) Properly adjust your attitude, going in. Be motivated to discover the truth. Many people enter an argument motivated only by a need to be proven right; to win a word-battle. A large number of people are resigned to this dangerous notion that paves only a path toward resentment and contributes to a further breakdown of communication. It's a self-esteem issue and often leads to saying hurtful things or bringing up irrelevant details to derail the opponent's train of thought. Be brave enough to uncover the truth, even if it means you were wrong.

2) Discuss, rather than argue. A fight, by definition, involves emotion, but if you can keep your tone of voice respectful and your arguments logical, then hurt feelings generated by the discussion will not obscure the issue. If you wouldn't use such language or tones of voice with a co-worker, you should resist using it with your partner.

3) Take turns. Do not talk until your partner has finished speaking. If you are constantly interrupting, then you are not listening. If you think that you know exactly what your partner is going to say, then you are listening to a voice inside your head, not your partner.

If you find that you are doing most of the talking, then you should consider the possibility that you are engaged in a monologue, rather than a dialogue. You can learn nothing new from a monologue. Your partner needs to contribute. Be sure to grant them ample time to compose thoughtful responses.

4) Neither of you are mind readers. Resist jumping to conclusions about your partner's thought processes. Since you are not a mind reader, you can have no idea what your partner truly thinks, except through what they tell you. Accept as fact what they say about their thoughts and motivations. Also, remember that the reverse is true: They cannot read your mind, so it's not fair to use the words "you should have known," unless you explicitly told them.

5) Timing: Discuss an incident as soon as possible after it occurs. The longer you wait, the more likely your memories will diverge. In the end, it will be a stand-off between your fading memories and theirs. My general rule is that the issue is dead if it hasn't been addressed within seven days.

6) Silence is Relationship Kryptonite. Complete and eternal silence is utterly destructive and should not be allowed. However, no one should be forced to supply immediate answers. Requiring snappy comebacks gives an unfair advantage to the quickest thinker. To arrive at the truth, a discussion must be fair.

There are those who seek emotional space by not speaking and while it's true that they are impeding intimacy, some allowance must be made for our human natures: Some are bold while others are skittish. In the same way that you wouldn't charge a shy kitten, neither should you relentlessly attack an emotionally timid partner. The fact that they have no quick answers does not mean that they are wrong.

Give your partner a break to regroup, to sort things out and to establish some comfort zone.

This is especially true in heated and emotional disagreements where hasty words may be regretted for a lifetime. If one of you wants time to think, accommodate this need without resentment.

Take a break, but make an appointment to return to the subject as soon as possible. Twenty-four hours would be a reasonable maximum, for most common squabbles. Each day that goes by, memories fade, making the discussion that much more difficult.

7) Stick to the subject. Wandering off topic is the typical strategy of someone who wants to obscure an issue. If a tangential subject comes up, write that down. Come back to it another day. No matter how harshly it has been introduced, resist the temptation to rebut. It's a trap. If you are in a discussion with someone whose only motivation is to win, they will try to lure you on to side topics with what appear to be easily refuted accusations. Once you go there, they feel safer and will often use semantics to invalidate your answer.

8) Don't Play the Semantics Game. Another common obfuscating tactic is the use of semantics: Your opponent focuses on insufficiencies in language to bury the logic of your argument. You know you're being pulled in this direction when you find yourself endlessly defining terms, in order to clarify your simplest statements.

Spoken language is inherently imprecise. Focus on the *intended* meaning of your partner's words, not the sentence structure.

9) Apologize. A sincere apology is never a bad thing. Receiving and apology helps your partner let go of their anger and resentment, which helps them to forgive. It also helps you learn. Humans learn little from success. Our most important lessons come from failure, and accepting responsibility. Even if you win an argument and get an apology, it is always a wise idea to look for any blame that might be yours. If you find some, you will learn something.

What constitutes a sincere apology…

- An apology is best done with words. Written words are the most powerful.
- If your apology is sincere, you'll probably feel uncomfortable and reluctant.
- Sending gifts is ok, but needs to be backed up with action and/or words.
- A proper apology does not contain mitigating words like "but" or "however."
- If you do not make yourself apologize properly, you are getting off too easily.
- The lower the quality of the apology, the less the value and, therefore, the less the effect.

10) Accept apologies gracefully. Sincerely apologizing hurts our pride and is a difficult thing to do. In fact, if we didn't value you and the relationship, we would never do it. You should view any apology as an indication of how much your partner cares. Don't gloat, and, above all, resist any temptation to add some parting shots to the discussion. Such behavior only makes apologizing more difficult and therefore, less likely.

If you accept the apology, you must forgive the transgression. Forgiving means accepting that your partner is sorry for what they have done. It also means accepting that they are making an honest effort to avoid repeating the behavior.

Ok, then. Let the games begin!

33

Sex, Drugs, Pets, and Gardens

Dude! You got'ta unthink that thought. Immediately!

I'm different.

I've been told this too many times to ignore.

But, by and large, I'm only different inside my own head. On the exterior, I'm extremely usual. Boringly so, in fact.

On the off chance that you might need to hear some of the things I do not say at work, in elevators, coffee dates, parties—really, anywhere that someone might actually hear them—I boldly present some of my slightly-left-of-center reasoning and observations on Drugs, Sex, Gardening and Pet Ownership, despite the fact that no good has ever come from me sharing what I truly think.

Using Drugs is Bad:

A long time ago, I heard a prominent practitioner of Chinese medicine being interviewed on the radio. When asked to give his best advice, he said, simply, "Don't get sick!" I chuckled, but then the longer I thought about this, the more brilliant it seemed.

Most of my family members have been long-lived, but my grandmother was an outstanding example. At eight-five, she looked sixty-five and was very active, mostly in her garden, several hours each day. Then she tripped and fell against a glass cabinet and got a shard of glass lodged in her hip. She was in great physical shape, so the operation did not take much out of her—but the recovery, that was a different story. She was instructed to stay off her feet for at least three months; advice she strictly adhered to. But afterwards, to the surprise of us all, she was never really active again! Like Dorian Gray, she aged, seemingly overnight, and spent her final ten years hobbling from her bed to her chair, within the confines of her house.

"Don't get sick," connects to a concept that I have always believed in: Balance. And the two things I believe about Balance are: (1) That it is comprised of both positive and negative, and (2) it is delicate. In terms of medicine: (1) The more effective the cure for one system, the more destructive it will be for another, and (2) once you artificially correct a system, it is difficult to restore the natural balance.

As I age, the proof seems to surround me. Many of my older friends and relatives grew up in an era when western medicine was revered and so they didn't think twice about popping a pill to fight discomfort, let alone actual pain. By the time they were my age, they were on multiple prescription medicines and some of them now have

issues with their livers that are most likely linked to the amount of drugs they've consumed. They've lived long lives, but I believe that they would be living their last years in better shape had they been more careful with their consumption of pharmaceuticals.

I am a believer in western medicine, but I was never one to take a pill if I could avoid it. I never wanted my body to build any tolerance to, or dependency on, a drug. This way, if I really *had* to take a pill, I hoped that its effectiveness would be maximized, and the negative impact on my body minimized.

This is not to say that I strictly practice what I preach.

"Medicine" is just a subcategory of "things we ingest" and I know that I should apply all of this, equally, to soda pop and potato chips, but sadly I find this a struggle. I do believe that junk food is anti-medicine and it causes imbalance in all the ways I avoid by not taking actual medicine, but, for me, there is one outrageously strong argument in favor of junk food: "It's freak'in delicious."

Now that I think about it, most of my larger problems start with my tongue.

Well, we all have to die of something.

Using Illegal Drugs is Worse:

I've long believed that laws create more criminals and victims than they eliminate, and the "War on Drugs" is a prime example.

I recently watched Michael Moore's, *"Where To Invade Next?"* (2015), a documentary in which he examines several areas in which the US lags behind other nations. At one point he made the observation that at about the time that black people gained power in the United States, Reagan began his "War on Drugs." The end product of this campaign was to put one third of black men into jails, in the southern states. In most states, once a person is incarcerated they lose their voting rights, for life. Thus, the right for black people to vote was dealt a blow. Meanwhile, the prison system routinely offers their inmates as cheap labour for powerful corporations. Because the prison population is now predominantly black and prisoners work for slave wages, essentially, black people in the United States have once again been stripped of their rights and made slaves!

The criminal justice system is factory churning out a lot of products, among which justice is a low-run, low quality item.

I wish all drugs were legal, worldwide. This would instantly delete so much crime and abuse that it could only be a good thing. I see no moral issue with adults "doing drugs," though I've never been a fan of drugs of any kind.

When I was younger I avoided illegal drugs mostly out of fear. I was unjustifiably proud of my brain and didn't want to take "mind-altering" substances precisely because they might alter my mind. It has since been strongly suggested to me that a little mind-altering would have done me some good.

Be that as it may, drugs held little attraction as I am easily amused and thoroughly satisfied by ordinary life. There have always been more than enough distractions to amuse me and I never really had much of an urge, beyond mild curiosity, to try drugs. And now, what, with Netflix and all...

I'm sure you've heard all the standard arguments against illegal drugs, but here's the one that people don't seem to expect and that instantly careens a rock'in party smack into an awkward pause whenever someone insists that I tell them why I don't do illegal drugs: Because, purchasing illegal drugs is a bad thing, purely because it's illegal.

All of your spending is a form of endorsement. In the case of illegal drugs, you are endorsing the worst elements in our society: very directly contributing to violence and abuse. And for what? A good time.

If everyone stopped purchasing illegal drugs, a large percentage of crime would disappear overnight. Personally, I could never justify putting money into that system, regardless of what I think about the unfairness of the legal system.

Crickets. Every time.

Owning Pets is Bad:

There are the two major reasons that I do not have pets: (1) I really love animals and (2) I want to be a considerate neighbor.

I love animals, but I haven't wanted to visit a zoo since the 1980's when I looked a gorilla in the eyes and immediately recognized that it was intelligent, massively bored and pretty pissed off at being kept in a cage. Sensitized by that experience, I then noticed that the large predators spent their day neurotically pacing, the elephants swaying. I went, once, to Sea World and was immediately struck by the fact that the whales were so large while their tanks were so small. Wild Orcas can swim 30 mph and 100 miles per day, yet live their captive lives in Olympic-swimming-pool-sized cages where they develop crippling diseases and sociopathic tendencies. I'm no biologist, but even to me, caging such animals is obvious cruelty. I have not set foot inside a zoo since the early nineties.

When I was young, I was a mini-zoo keeper, blinded by human-centric views and a sense of entitlement to every element on the planet. I had mice, rats, gerbils, rabbits, a ferret, a dog, cats, lizards and fish. The reason I had so many is that they died... often. I tried to take good care of them, but I was too young, the learning curve too gradual, and the animals too small and delicate. My ignorance and carelessness meant a constant turn over. Only the cats and dog survived well because they were more resilient, and largely cared for by my parents.

It took me an especially long time to get over the death of my dog, but I loved every one of my pets.

It's a common notion that every caring person loves animals. They love their innocence, their cuddliness, their unconditional return of affection. They consider pets a member of the family. If you don't have a pet, you are dead inside, and possibly a sociopath.

But the lesson that my pets eventually taught me was: Do not keep animals as pets. My love for my pets was a human-centric, inconsiderate type of love—the same love I see exhibited by many pet owners; especially in the city. Many do not take pet ownership seriously enough, treating animals like emotional toys instead of living beings with an equal right to the best life possible. They spoil them in human-centric ways; buying knitted scarves or gold-plated food dishes. It's as misguided as a husband getting his wife a vacuum cleaner for Valentine's Day, though less dangerous.

"Nope," Pet by Pet...

Dogs: Dogs are the ones I feel most sorry for because they are so guileless, loving and loyal. Dogs need to run. The larger the dog, the larger the run they need. A half-hour walk to the local park and back, once a day, does not come close to satisfying a dog's need for exercise. Also, making them wait half a day to go to the bathroom is unkind; doubly so if they are punished when they fail to hold it. As well, dogs are keenly attached to their pack members, especially the alpha dog— you. When you are not there, they pine. If you are away from home a lot and/or don't live in the wide-open countryside, then a dog is not going to have the life it deserves. On balance, your love is extremely valuable to a dog. But you are forcing them to exchange some of their own health and happiness for that love.

Cats: From an animal-cruelty point of view, having a cat is not an impractical choice, but you, alone, do not "own" your cat. The entire neighborhood "owns" your cat because cats wander and yowl and deposit their poop wherever they please. Again, in the countryside, this outside animal can lead a comfortable, healthy life, and you will "own" your cat there because no one else will have to deal with it.

Rodents: I'm willing to admit that I see little wrong with owning this variety of pet. But, still, I generally observe that the cages are

"He's one of the family," she said.

"Well, that must have tickled," I thought.

made to maximize viewing and minimize recapture time, and do not provide enough space for the activity levels of these animals. A running wheel is no walk in the park.

Birds: How would you feel if you could fly, but instead, were relegated to a two-foot cage? Think that your pet would choose to stay with you, over freedom? What do you think would happen if you didn't clip its wings, put the cage outside and left the cage door open? What does this tell you?

Fish: I think these are the pets that we torture the least because of their size and limited brain power, but they are no less abused. Fish are small and delicate: One second, they seemed to be floating a little off-center, and the next, they are floating upside-down. If you think about the massive numbers that a pet shop stocks on any given day of the year, you will realize that it reflects the massive number of fish that die as pets.

Reptiles: Maybe. But, like fish, they tend to die easily and like rodents, cages small enough to give us easy access are too small to provide a full life for the animal.

Spiders and Spider-like Creatures: We once had a red-backed jumping spider crawling around the house, for about two weeks. I didn't kill it or remove it because I thought, "even though it's creepy-looking, we can co-exist. What a great life lesson for the kids." Then, one day, it crawled into her bed sheets and savagely bit my daughter on the finger. Her finger went numb and arm ached for three days. I almost died from lack of sleep, checking on her every two hours, during the night. Still, I didn't kill the spider. Instead, I gingerly carried it outside where I hope something else would kill the mean-spirited little bastard! Spiders, you had your chance and you blew it, big time. So, nope!

Dangerous Animals: I find it absurd that a person can own an exotic animal that is in any way dangerous to a human being. I mean: Why does one person's impulse to cuddle a python outweigh his neighbor's personal safety? Why?!

Gardening—Could be Good, but Mostly Bad:

I never thought that I would, but I've come to enjoy gardening.

I like the creativity of designing yard-scapes, though I'm not very good at it. Moreover, I like the activity level—just enough to keep my body happy without monopolizing my mind; I get exercise and am still able to contemplate life or that last episode of Breaking Bad.

But my quirky mind seems to enjoy spoiling my own fun.

One day, while schlepping wheelbarrows of topsoil, I suddenly realized that, like owning an exotic pet, gardening requires a huge support-industry geared towards making things grow where they otherwise could not. I looked at my little garden filled with rocks blasted out of a distant quarry, soil scraped from some river delta, fertilizer composed of elements from the far reaches of the periodic table and the globe, and seeds cultivated in foreign greenhouses, and it instantly occurred to me that I was assembling a large, exotic terrarium—completely artificial, unsustainable, perpetually out of balance and costly. And because I suck at it: ultimately not worth the effort.

A gardener has a lot in common with Sisyphus.

My meager attempts at beautifying my world were actually destroying it. All those elements, all that refining and shipping, were gouging chunks of real beauty out of the earth, grinding them down and burning fossil fuels to haul them to my doorstep where I then expended great effort in transforming them into faded echoes of nature.

And, all of this because someone, somewhere, decided to label some plants as "weeds."

I'm still trying to figure out what indigenous plants will grow in my indigenous hard-packed clay and how I can obtain and nurture those plants. Paradoxically, not many native plants can be found in a local nursery. Those "weeds" have been shipped to another land where they are considered "flowers." As well, it is no longer easy to know what is native. Most of the things that spring up on their own are invasive foreigners. I'd build a wall if I could figure out how to make the weeds pay for it.

My ultimate garden would be one in which the dandelions grow, but are kept in check by other native plants. I have no idea what that might look like but have a feeling my neighbors would not be on board. They have little to fear. My patch is relatively small and surrounded by exotic terrariums blooming with of non-native plants, so my new dream garden is likely unachievable.

I used to love animals but hate the rain.

Then, I started gardening and realized how misguided that was. Now I appreciate all kinds of weather because of what it does for the plants.

...and I hate rabbits, racoons, deer, squirrels and most birds.

wmdean.com

Also, as a gardener, I suck. The only reason my thumb is green at all is because it's envious of other thumbs.

Emotion, Sex, Love, Relationships—All Good...Usually

I like to dissect complicated concepts, breaking them into their simplest component parts, if I can. Here's where I'm at with relationships and emotion.

- Ultimately, we are descendants of prey, and we are all still afraid. Thus, ultimately, most of our life choices are spurred by fear.

- Our deepest emotions evolve from comfort zones established in childhood and, later, refined by adult experience. Comfort zones are psychological zones of apparent relative safety, arising as a response to fear.

- Emotion exists to disentangle our brains from decision-making equations that we cannot balance. Defining "good" and "bad" requires a point of view or an agenda. A point of view/agenda requires a bias. This bias is emotion. It keeps us from decision-paralysis by tipping the scales when there is no "best" answer.

- Love boils down to a feeling of invulnerability and, thus, an exceptional lack of fear. At full force, it is a deep belief in a righteous purpose, which fills a person with such satisfaction that it overrides all fear, even that presented by mortal peril. A person thus satisfied in death, is thereby satisfied with life.

  As a practical example: Many people would gladly take a bullet to save their child. They can do this because love fills them with a clarity of purpose that society unanimously endorses, providing the ultimate validation. The conviction that such a death would have a deep meaning and is clearly the "right" thing to do overrides all fear. In normal life, when death is not imminent, this righteous feeling can fuel and justify many aggressive and risky behaviors. This is why parents will stand up for their children in circumstances where they might never stand up for themselves.

- There is no such thing as a soul mate.

  I'm going to say it again: There is no such thing as a soul mate.

  I repeated this because the soul mate thing is such a commonly accepted myth that it's almost heresy to speculate otherwise. But no single person can give you everything you will ever crave. The reason for this is that humans want everything, and spend their lives trying to get as much of it as they can. Everyone has to compromise because it's impossible to have everything, if for no other reason than that some things are mutually exclusive: If she's black, she can't also be white; if he's ripped, he can't also be a couch potato.

  Moreover, there is no one who can "complete you." And no one wants to. Complete yourself, then you'll be a better catch for the kind of person you want to be with.

  Whether or not you think that I'm right about this, take a moment to consider the ways in which the soul mate idea sabotages the average person's love life. When you're dating, the idealized soul mate fiction makes it difficult to settle for a real person. When you are in a relationship, believing that somewhere out there your soul mate is waiting is a distraction and a relationship-sinking thought that will occur every time your expectations are not met. Abandoning the idea of a soul mate better prepares you to meet and maintain a relationship with an actual human being.

Of course, there are people who might inherently be easier to live with, long-term. But it doesn't matter how well you fit at first, that initial connection can only get you so far. Once you're living, day in and day out, in close quarters, it will take seriously hard work to maintain your relationship.

I always think of a relationship as a vehicle, because, as the song says, "Life is a highway." Your relationship might be a 1994 Ford Aerostar but, at first, while you're speeding along fresh asphalt, it's going to drive like a brand new Ferrari. The problem is the more roads you travel, the more likely you'll reach a stretch that's not paved. And sometimes, you're going to have to go off-road. And for that, you're going to need an all-terrain vehicle with snow tires and a winch. The real question is: How hard are you both willing to work to adapt your vehicle? Or to put it another way: "How A-Team are you?"

- Related to the previous point: Coincidence exists. What many refer to as "Fate" is simply a romantic notion built upon the inadequacy of our human minds to properly evaluate statistical chance.

- Sex is a physical mechanism that aids bonding by easily generating instant feelings of validation and intimacy, even where none exists. Obviously, the sex act is essential for reproduction, but the sex drive is essential for genetic diversity by encouraging people to experiment outside of their social spheres.

  Sex is an intimate physical act and it is dangerous in many ways to enter into a sexual relationship carelessly, however, it is also dangerous to believe that there is a direct connection between sex and love. A piece of bad advice that is commonly passed from generation to generation is that you should only have sex with people if you are in love—or worse, married. The problem with instilling this belief is that while a youngster is learning to cope with overpowering sexual urges, there is a good chance that they will "fall in love" with the sexiest person they meet, just to morally justify getting laid. Taking the emotion out of the equation will simplify and clarify their choices.

- Romance is a vivid emotional illusion that there is a special bond between people. There are many mechanisms which can create and strengthen this bond and many which can dissolve it. Because it is just a feeling, it can exist even where not appropriate.

  Actively participating in mutually acceptable romantic activities strengthens the emotional bond between two people. It is an artificial thing and cannot exist without the effort of the people involved, but the emotional bond it creates is a comfort zone, useful in maintaining a long-term relationship.

- Intimacy is relative. There is no "right way" to be intimate and what is intimate to one person may be intrusive to another. At one end of the scale is Mr. Spock (representing embarrassment) and, at the other end, a Stalker (representing insecurity). Think about where on this graph your intimacy preferences would fall. Now think about where your partner should appear on the graph. If the gap between you is small, then you are lucky and probably very satisfied with this aspect of your relationship. If the gap is large, it's probably best to learn to accept their nature. There is no good/right or bad/wrong, and there are advantages and disadvantages to every position on the graph— other than the extremes. The real problem is the gap.

  One good exercise is to image yourself in a relationship with someone at the extreme end of your side of the graph. If you tend to be reserved with your feelings, then imagine being with an excessively disciplined person who shows no emotion and has taken a vow of silence. If you are the more expressive type, then imagine your partner is a stalker who constantly nags you for every detail of your every thought and action. You will probably feel some degree of embarrassment or insecurity. This should give you some idea what your partner might feel whenever you nudge them to close the intimacy gap.

- The single biggest thing that people want from their relationships is validation. It's why people are attracted to people that they feel might be "out of their league," and why continuing to feel appreciated is such a large thing in a long-term relationship of any kind. It's also why a sudden decrease in a partner's social status adversely affects the relationship. Praise from someone of lower status has lower value.

- Appreciating and feeling appreciated is a huge element in all relationships.

One common trap for people is to expend effort in areas that the other person doesn't consider important. A classic example is always doing the dishes while your partner lets them pile up.

You consider it important and each time you wash them, you think that you're doing a favor for your partner. Rightly or wrongly, your partner considers the dishes a low priority or else they wouldn't let them pile up, or they consider doing dishes a trivial task, otherwise they wouldn't let you do them alone, every time.

Left unaddressed, you will grow resentful that your efforts go unrecognized.

So, who's wrong?

Mostly you, if you allow this to persist.

You are the one in the best position to alter this cycle of under appreciation and resentment because you are definitely aware of it and you are actively contributing to the situation. Expecting your partner to spontaneously appreciate something that is of little value to them is unrealistic. Feeling sorry for yourself is a signal that you are doing something wrong. In order to address your feelings of under appreciation you need to do something, or stop doing something. Either way, it is within your own power.

Playing the martyr is a refusal to acknowledge your own role in the dynamic while setting a trap for your partner to fall into in order to justify your feelings of under appreciation.

"Do, or do not," but don't expect others to appreciate gifts they do not value.

If you've tried everything you can think of to address this issue and the situation persists, your final choice is to rethink your own priorities. If you are unable to change your mindset, then you are free to nurture your inner martyr. But realize that martyrdom is a dull knife to a relationship. The longer it lasts, the deeper the gouge.

- Empathy is an essential ingredient for all long-term relationships.
  When empathy runs out, the relationship runs aground.

- Relationships are a lot more fragile than people generally believe.

- Love, sex and romance are all good for your physical and mental health, though falling in love with a serial killer provides only short-term benefits.

Thank you for hearing me out. And don't worry—I find your nervous glances endearing and now realize how much less awkward it is being me, than being the person standing next to me.

Sex, Violence, and Santa

34

WARNING!
CHRISTMAS MAGIC SPOILERS!
DO NOT LET YOUR CHILDREN READ THIS!

Before I became a parent, I decided never to lie to my children. Yes, I can hear you laughing.

I wasn't going to lie about sexual things or violence because I remembered that when I was young, many things that adults considered shocking never shocked me. As a child, I lacked the emotional depth to even see the shocking element within adult situations.

Most people lie to their children about sex and are panic-stricken when their child comes across pornographic images—hard to avoid, these days. I don't bring the subject up, but if my child asks a question, then I assume he/she is old enough to handle the answer. I do try to be as detached and clinical as possible. So long as you stick to answering only the question that was asked, the awkward follow-up question rarely comes.

One afternoon, I made the mistake of typing the words "Canadian Beaver" into a search engine. After asking me what that man was doing to that woman, I waited for my six-year-old to ask me if I had ever done that with Mommy. But, his next question was about lunch. ADHD, it seems, is a built-in safety feature designed to protect the psyche of young children.

If a prepubescent child happens to see pornography, they understand it only in terms of things they've experienced. Mostly, they think naked people are funny. They do not understand any of the negative things about such images. A parent's reaction to such images, however, has a very large impact. If you get flustered your kids will notice and will reframe the image as offensive and shameful, though they won't understand why. You will be perpetuating embarrassment and shame for another generation.

I'm not saying that kids (or anyone, really) should be encouraged to consume porn. The average preteen will have little interest. And once the hormones hit, I think parental guidance is required to lend perspective and reduce the long-term negative effects that idealized and objectified sexual images have on attitudes and expectations.

Oddly, most people seem more concerned with sex and less concerned with the violence to which their children are exposed. I do not agree with children freely consuming violence in video games, TV or movies. Violent imagery can be scary and desensitizing. But it's not a simple thing. Bugs Bunny and Roadrunner are silly and kids know that it is not real. They do not get scared, nor do they begin to plot hanging a ten-ton anvil above the snack machine, at school. Well, some might. But I say if they can lift a ten-ton anvil, then they can pretty much do whatever they want.

At the other end of the scale from Road Runner cartoons, an adult horror movie is made to be chillingly real. The violence looks more realistic and is emotionally staged so that you relate to the characters. Small children will be frightened to think that such things actually happen, or will become desensitized, believing that such things are relatively routine and less important/shocking than they actually are. Either way, it skews an otherwise natural development toward the negative. And, I don't think that words from a parent can eliminate the negative effects. It's emotional, beyond the reach of words.

So, my parenting plan was that I would curb my children's exposure to violent images, not worry about porn and never lie about anything. Most especially, I wasn't going to lie about such trivial things as the Tooth Fairy, Easter Bunny and Santa Claus. But, like many of my plans, it bore little resemblance to what followed.

I have never understood why we will tell our children not to take candy from strangers then promote trick or treating. We teach our kids that telling the truth is always best and then lie to them about Santa and the Easter Bunny.

When legitimate news organizations started Santa-tracking via satellite, I was appalled by how far adults will go to perpetuate the fantasy that a jolly, giant (for an elf) flies around the earth in twenty-four hours on a reindeer-powered snow sled that must travel at near-light speeds.

Lying to kids is now an industry. You can pay people to send fake Santa letters to your kids. You can type their vitals into a website which will generate a personalized Santa video. Even the government's in on it. Write a letter to Santa and the post office will generate a reply. If you've never believed in government conspiracies, now you know it's possible.

Why do parents do this? To see the smiling, deluded faces of innocent children? It's like leading a rabbit into the slaughterhouse with a carrot. The illusion is unsustainable and hobbling to their development of reason.

But that's not why parents do this.

They do this because all the other parents do this and if you don't, then your kid will become a pariah.

Kids tend to blurt out whatever they are thinking and if your kid's the one telling the others that Santa isn't real, he/she will be the Typhoid Mary of Peace, Joy and Happiness throughout the holiday season. Parents will not let their children be exposed to your child. Very quickly, your child's only friends will be imaginary. And the next thing you know you're setting an extra plate at the dinner table for "Mr. Sniggles."

I don't want to have to lie about Mr. Sniggles. On the other hand, I don't want to be the one breaking the bad news to little anime-eyed innocents. My sister still harbors trauma from forty years ago when our uncle folded up her imaginary friend and threw him in the garbage can.

And that's why I lie to my children.

Please help!

I'd kill to get a review on Amazon.com.
But I'm really hoping it doesn't come to that.
Please help by taking a minute to go online
and write an honest review.

Thank you for your purchase,
and for reading my book.
I hope you enjoyed it.

More From William M Dean

I Married Japan:
Japan's hilarious journey into one man's life

Think you just married an exotic Japanese woman? Wrong! In fact, you just married all of exotic Japan and 3000 years of history. But, the die is cast, the adventure's begun, and the wonders and wondering will never cease. Throw in a couple of kids and a quirky Canadian family filled with characters, and you have the makings of epic tragedy, or gut-busting comedy, depending upon your point of view.

Get ready to learn, and be prepared to laugh your way through this collection of Japan-related articles on family life with the Deans!

The Space between Thought
a novel of love, life, death, tea, and time travel

Simon Sykes has money and power. He has Celeste; a beautiful, talented and devoted girlfriend. And, secretly, he has his pick of other women, on the side.

But Celeste's sudden death deals him a staggering blow and Simon vows to uncover the truth, at any cost.

While his business languishes and friends grow concerned for his sanity, Simon stumbles upon a secret that promises the power to unravel the mystery and undo one life-altering moment—the power to save Celeste and restore his future: Time travel.

Meanwhile, Simon's suspicious behavior has renewed police interest in the case. With Chief Inspector Holloway closing in, Simon wrestles with time, space and reality to rescue the love of his life, unmask her true killer and remodel his world.

The Book of 5 Uncredible Short Stories
from the distorted mind of William M. Dean

If, all of your life, you have been desperately seeking a book filled with aliens, maniacal sheep, cupids and other mythical creatures—then your life is sad and you are misguided, to say the least. However, luck is with you and within these pages you will find far-fetched stories from far-flung realities, told with exaggeration that amplifies truths, and adjectives that modify nouns.

This is a work of fiction and has been scrupulously edited to exclude all fact so as not to distract from all those aliens, maniacal sheep, cupids and postal workers you were looking for.

For the rest of you, there is at least one stunningly good-looking woman and some cute cats.

Discover more at: https://www.wmdbooks.com

Also, available at amazon.com/author/wmdbooks
and other fine book retailers.